For manuscript enquiries, contact: amy@thecluelessclub.com

For illustration enquiries, contact: lauren@thecluelessclub.com

The members of the Clueless Club are works of fiction. Unless otherwise indicated, all the names, characters, places, events and incidents in this book are either the product of the author's imagination or used in a fictitious manner. Any resemblance to actual persons, living or dead, or actual events is purely coincidental.

As for the crew of the Mary Celeste and the Dei Gratia – all are based on the real people involved but the interpretations and narrative in this book are entirely fictional. The imagined crew members in the opening chapter do, however, abide by the generally agreed-upon facts from the time and have been drawn from primary sources and documents, including first-hand accounts and testimony from the investigation held following the discovery of the abandoned ship.

Book Cover and illustrations: Lauren Woodley

Typesetting: A. A. Roskilly

1st edition, 2024

Printed in the UK

THE CLUELESS CLUB

Takes on
THE MARY CELESTE

Written by
A. A. Roskilly

Illustrated by
Lauren Woodley

For my girls
Hero, Persephone and Hebe
xxx

Welcome to the Clueless Club!

Every Friday afternoon at Cinderbanks Primary School, just as everyone else is escaping for the weekend, Mr Lewes and the members of the Clueless Club gather to tackle some of history's greatest mysteries.

This week they're exploring the eerie disappearance of the crew and passengers of the sailing ship, the Mary Celeste.

Are you ready to join the club?

Mr Lewes is the Year Five teacher at Cinderbanks Primary School.

He loves history, is fascinated by mysteries and is also the leader of the Clueless Club.

← → MAX ← →

Age:
11

Favourite mystery:
The vanishing
lighthouse keepers of
Eilean Mor

About Max:

Max has a bit
of a reputation
for getting into
trouble at school,
but it never seems
to follow him into
the Clueless Club
classroom.

He burns off
his energy on the
football and hockey
pitch and loves
dramatic mysteries
with lots of fighting
and maybe even a
little bloodshed.

GWEN

⟵   GWEN   ⟶

Age:

9

Favourite mystery:

The lost colony of
Roanoke Island

About Gwen:

The newest member of
the Clueless Club, Gwen
has only just started
at Cinderbanks
Primary so is a bit of
a mystery herself.

However, she's not
afraid to be different
and when it comes to
mysteries, for her, it's
the crazier the better!

You can count on
Gwen to bring the
most unbelievable and
the most outlandish
theories to the club.

← FREDDIE →

Age:

10

Favourite mystery:

The Loch Ness Monster

About Freddie:

Freddie might have a reputation as the class clown, but he's also kind, fun-loving and adventurous.

He's interested in just about everything, but most especially monsters and mythical creatures of all kinds.

He loves nothing more than some kind of terrifying beastie bursting onto the scene and causing chaos.

Age:

10

Favourite mystery:

The disappearance of
Amelia Earheart

About Alice:

Alice's favourite topic
at school is science. She
loves reading about the
natural world and space
and enjoys carrying out
wild experiments in her
kitchen.

She has a keen attention
to detail and in the
Clueless Club her
theories are always backed
up with plenty of evidence.

←— **You** —→

Age:

_____

Favourite mystery:

_____

_____

About You:

_____

_____

_____

_____

_____

_____

_____

_____

THE MARY CELESTE

Fold here
so you can find
your way back to
the glossary easily!

A two-masted brigantine cargo ship, the Mary Celeste was used to transport goods for sale between North America and Europe.

GLOSSARY

- **Binnacle:** A waist-high stand to hold a compass

- **Cargo:** Goods carried by a ship

- **Cleat:** T-shaped metal or wood to which ropes can be tied

- **Figurehead:** A carving at the prow of the ship

- **Galley:** The kitchen area on a ship or an aircraft

- **Hold:** The space for carrying cargo below deck

- **Hull:** The main body of a ship or boat

- **Prow:** The pointed front part of the ship

- **Scabbard:** A cover for a sword, often made of leather

- **Vessel:** A ship or large boat

Benjamin Briggs, Sarah and Sophia

← THE CREW OF THE MARY CELESTE →

Andrew	Edward	Volkert	Boz	Gotlieb	Albert	Arian
2nd Mate	Cook	Seaman	Seaman	Seaman	1st Mate	Seaman
Danish	American	German	German	German	American	German

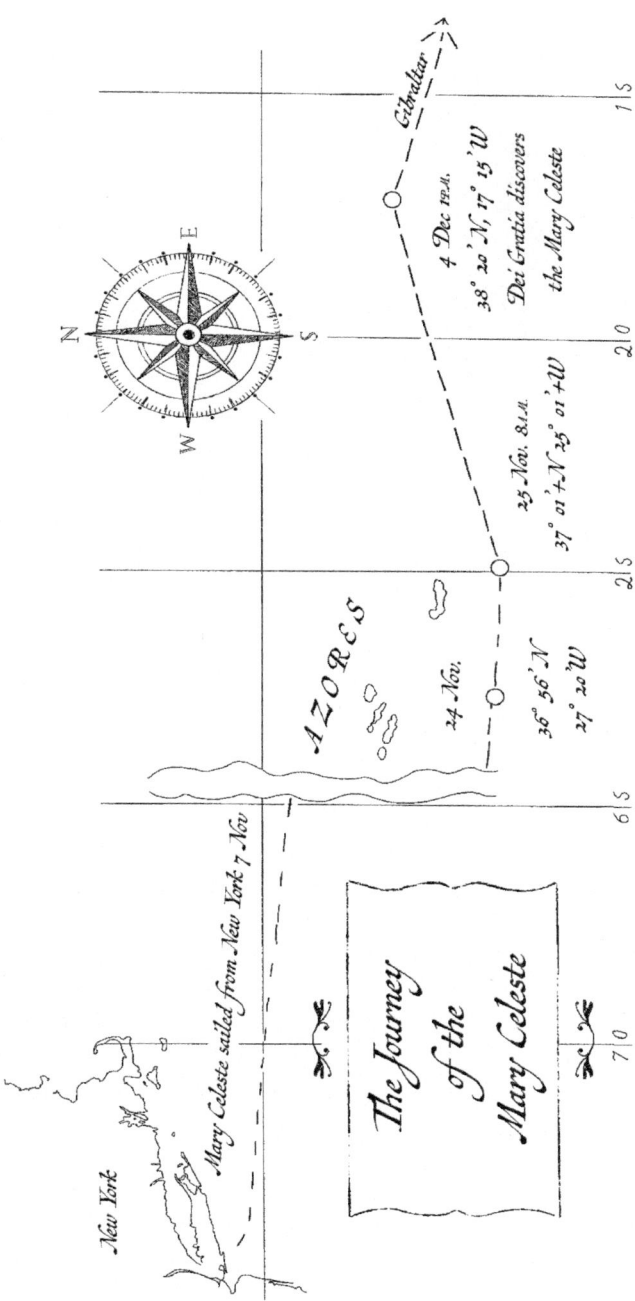

The Journey
of the
Mary Celeste

New York

Mary Celeste sailed from New York 7 Nov

AZORES

24 Nov.
36° 56' N
27° 20' W

25 Nov. 8 a.m.
37° 01' N, 25° 01' W

4 Dec 1872
38° 20' N, 17° 15' W
Dei Gratia discovers
the Mary Celeste

Gibraltar

N
E
S
W

9

1
JOIN THE CLUB

The worst bit about mysteries is not knowing. That was why they had all joined the club; they couldn't take the fact there might not be an answer and they were determined to find one.

It was Friday afternoon and kids were flooding out of the gates of Cinderbanks Primary School, heading home for a weekend of fun and ignoring their homework for as long as they could get away with.

That was all except Freddie, Max, and Alice. They stayed behind after everyone else had gone, as they always did on a Friday. They gathered outside the Year Five classroom, and peered through the open door.

"Come in guys," Mr Lewes said, setting a large pile of books on a shelf and waving them in.

They dumped their bags along the wall and pulled out chairs, dragging them to the front of the classroom. Freddie, with his stand-up hair and lunch-stained jumper, bounced on to his seat excitedly. Beside him sat the blonde-haired Max, whose reputation for being the bad kid never seemed to follow him into Mr Lewes' room. On the far end sat Alice, her thick brown hair pulled back into a neat plait, her uniform somehow still perfect and her eyes wide with enthusiasm.

"We're just waiting for one more," Mr Lewes said as they all sat down.

"A new member?" Alice asked.

They'd been a trio all term; Mr Lewes' club certainly wasn't for kids who thought they were "cool". Before anyone could ask another question, the door swung open and silhouetted against the lights of the hall outside stood a girl. Her hair was tied back in messy bunches that looked as if they were barely hanging on. She had a bag slung over her left shoulder and the sleeves of her jacket fell down over her hands. The children turned in their seats to stare.

"Welcome to the Clueless Club, Gwen!" Mr Lewes said brightly. "Grab a seat and we'll get started."

Alice gave Gwen a welcoming smile and shuffled her chair aside to make a space, eager for things to begin.

"The way things work at the Clueless Club, Gwen, is that we investigate a mystery each week, and it's your job to put forward a theory about what happened. We'll discuss all the theories as we go and see if we can agree on which one is the most likely. This week we're looking at perhaps the most famous maritime mystery," Mr Lewes said, pointing to the image of an old-fashioned ship on the whiteboard. The ship had two tall masts and white sails billowing in the wind. It seemed to be drifting into an unknown distance upon frozen, choppy seas.

"The Mary Celeste," said Gwen, leaning one arm casually over the back of her chair as she admired the ship.

"That's right," Mr Lewes smiled.

Four pairs of eyes looked back at him, alight with excitement. Alice could barely sit still.

"Let's dive right in! The year is 1872," Mr Lewes started, lowering his voice dramatically and reaching up to turn down the lights.

* * *

The merchant sailing ship, the Dei Gratia, was making its way towards Gibraltar from the United States. The voyage had been going smoothly, despite some rough seas, and Captain Morehouse was a happy man. That was, at least, until he heard a voice shouting down from the lookout: "Ship ahoy to Starboard!"

Captain Morehouse snatched up his binoculars and peered over the starboard railing. Dipping in and out of sight on the horizon, a tiny ship bobbed. It looked familiar. He ordered his crew to change course towards the vessel. Something felt strange. The ship was leaning slightly over, almost as though it was limping in the water. Some of the sails had been torn, the shreds billowing wildly in the wind.

"It's the Mary Celeste, Captain," the lookout shouted.

Morehouse looked through his binoculars again and this time he too could make out the tiny golden letters across the hull.

The Mary Celeste had left port days before the Dei Gratia had; she should have long since docked in Genoa by now. What was she doing here, floating as though wounded in the Atlantic Ocean?

"Signal them," he ordered. There was no reply.

"Something's not right, Captain," the lookout called again and this time there was a note of nervousness in his voice. "I can't see no one on deck. It's like she's sailing herself!"

As the Dei Gratia drew up alongside the Mary Celeste, the crew gathered along the rail watching the deserted ship warily. Her sails flapped lazily in the breeze, and she leant ever so slightly to the side, as if she was thinking of turning. Captain Morehouse turned towards his second in command, frowning.

"Deveau, take some men and board her," he said.

The first mate returned his grim expression. Deveau pointed at two of his crewmates and jerked his thumb towards the stricken ship.

"Thomas, John, with me," he said.

The Dei Gratia crew watched from the railing, chewing on their lips if they weren't chewing on their pipes, as the three men lowered themselves into a small rowing boat. With sweaty hands upon the oars, they rowed themselves across the short strip of water that separated the two vessels.

13

Deveau fastened the little boat against the side of the Mary Celeste. The ship loomed over them, a great shadowy beast without a master. One by one they climbed over the rail and set their feet down upon the gently rolling deck.

Deveau stood, his hands gripping the rail behind him, as though he were ready to turn and run at any moment. They gazed about the deserted deck. Above their heads the white sails fluttered and whipped like birds, some tattered and torn, some missing altogether. The huge sheet of canvas that made up the mainsail had been dropped and lay in a crumpled heap on the deck. Slowly, stepping with care amongst the coils of ropes and piles of canvas, Deveau crossed the deck.

"Sir!" The voice behind made him jump and with a cry of shock he spun about. At the back of the ship, standing in the shadow of an open sail, John and Thomas waved him over.

"Look here," John said, crouching down. In his hand he held a heavy rope.

Deveau followed the rope with his eyes as it trailed across the deck, the end of it wound and fixed tightly about an iron cleat. The other end ran out of sight over the rail. Deveau nodded and Thomas pulled on the rope, hand over hand, drawing it in. As the sodden rope was dragged from the water, it became increasingly tangled and woven with seaweed, as if it had been soaking in the water for days. Then, with a flick of water, the rope suddenly ended in a frayed and tattered mess.

"It's snapped," John said, looking up and holding the dripping end. "What was it attached to?"

Deveau rose and looked back across the deserted deck.

There was an empty space where the lifeboat would have been. He looked back at the broken rope with a frown.

"I think it was tied to the lifeboat," he murmured. "Come on."

They dropped the rope, thoughts and faces darkening, and picked their way across the deck. As they passed the main hatchway that led down into the hull of the ship, Deveau leant over and gave the handle a shake.

"Locked," he said.

"There," John pointed up ahead towards a smaller hatchway at the front of the ship. "That one's open."

"So it is," Deveau said, his frown deepening as he climbed over the remains of the mainsail and approached the open hatch, its cover laying upturned beside it. The three men looked at one another nervously.

"Looks like it's been blown off," Thomas said, but Deveau raised a hand to stop him.

"Don't. We don't know anything; we may yet find everyone below deck and then we can ask them."

Thomas and John exchanged grim and sceptical looks.

"Listen, Deveau..." John said.

Deveau paused, one elbow resting upon his knee, as he peered into the dark hatch and listened. Around them they could hear the endless spray of the waves sloshing against the hull of the ship. They could hear the tattered rigging slapping aimlessly against the masts. They could hear the gentle, tired creak of the wood. They were all sounds that, to the seasoned sailors, were as familiar and constant as their breath. The Mary Celeste sounded exactly as she should, except for one thing...

"Not a single voice," Deveau whispered. *No shouts and cries of the crew setting the sails, no bellowed orders from the captain over the roar of the waves, no eerie echo of sailors' songs, snatched away by the wind. The deck of the Mary Celeste was silent and lifeless. Maybe it was the chill of the Atlantic breeze, or maybe it was something more, but the hairs on the back of their necks prickled and rose.*

"Let's get this over with," Deveau said. *"The sooner we do the sooner we can get the hell off this ship."* The other two nodded and, with deep breaths, followed him down through the hatch.*

It took a moment for their eyes to adjust to the gloom below deck. The three of them hovered around the light of the open hatchway, too scared to move forward into the darkness. As soon as his eyes could make sense of the shadows, Deveau pushed himself away from the ladder and moved through the living space. As commander of this little expedition, it was his duty to lead his men and to at least pretend he wasn't afraid.

Below deck the eerie, alien silence was far worse. The wooden planks of the deck above muffled the comforting sounds of the sails and sea and left them feeling as though they were trapped below ground. Miners facing the darkness, and all that it held, alone.

They passed between the rows of hammocks, six swinging empty beds for the six members of the crew that weren't important enough to have their own cabins. Deveau paused, his eyes sweeping about the dingy space. He rested a hand against one of the hammocks.

"It's all still here. All their stuff," John said. *He was leaning forward between two of the hammocks and peering into a battered wooden chest. He dropped the lid with a crack that split the air and straightened up with a thin, polished*

pipe in his hand.

"Why'd they leave without their pipes?" he muttered darkly, a hand blindly reaching around to check that his own pipe was still safely in his pocket.

They exchanged looks. Why on earth had the Mary Celeste's sailors gone, leaving all their worldly possessions behind them?

As Deveau and Thomas made their way deeper into the shadows, John tossed the pipe on to the nearest hammock and hurried after them. He didn't want to be left alone on board this ghost ship.

They ducked beneath the ladder that led up to the locked main hatch and Deveau peered into the kitchen galley. The others watched as he examined the dark space. The others let out the breath they hadn't realised they were holding when Deveau turned and shook his head.

"Nothing," he said. "Let's go back up." He nodded towards the square of light that fell through the open hatch.

Relieved to be back out in the fresh air and the light, well away from the stifling silence below deck, Deveau crossed the boards and reached out to knock on the closed door of the captain's cabin. He knew there was likely no point in knocking, that there wouldn't be anyone inside to answer, but he couldn't shake the habit. As his knuckle rapped against the wood, the door creaked open, spilling light into the deserted room beyond. They moved inside and spread out to search the space.

Deveau approached the captain's desk. There were charts and maps scattered across the tabletop and many more had fluttered to the floor. As the ship listed gently in the swell an empty bottle rolled from one side of the room to the other, the noise startling in the creaking silence.

Everything, from the ceiling to the floor, was soaking wet with sea water. The ink on the maps had spread like a dark ocean across the damp paper. An oil lamp lay on its side, glass shattered, its flame long since doused. Deveau shuffled aside a pile of damp papers, they tore apart at his touch and fell with a splatter to the floor. Beneath was a heavy book, bound in red leather. He paused, his fingers resting on the front cover, tracing the golden letters that spelt out "Mary Celeste Log."

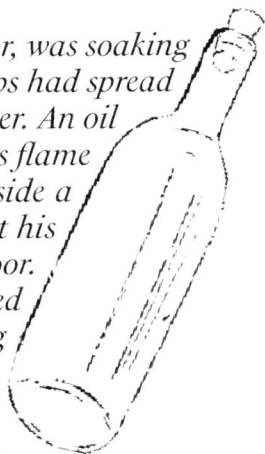

"What is it, Sir?" Thomas asked, stepping up behind him.

Deveau jumped and cried out. "It's the logbook," he snapped angrily.

"He left the logbook?" Thomas asked, confused. Surely that would be the first thing the captain would take as he prepared to abandon ship.

The spine of the book creaked as Deveau opened it, gingerly peeling the damp pages apart. He turned each one carefully until he reached the last entry. He ran his finger down the page, tracking the dates, noting the short comments from the captain about an otherwise uneventful trip. The last entry was marked the 25th November 1872.

"Ten days ago, sir..." Thomas whispered, reading over his shoulder.

Deveau flicked through the following pages, all of them empty. Then he flipped the book back to the start before opening each page again, more slowly this time, searching for any clues as to what possibly could have happened. There was nothing.

"It's like they just vanished," he murmured to himself.

A glint of metal above Thomas's head drew Deveau's eye and he saw, mounted on the damp wall, a narrow sword in its decorative scabbard. Deveau let the logbook fall shut and reached out a hand to take down the sword. The dampness in the room had seeped into the sheath and he had to fight in order to draw out the blade. He could see his own worried eyes reflected in the steel, but here and there the image was interrupted by a dark reddish-brown stain, splattered all along the blade.

"You don't think it's... blood?"

"No," Deveau said firmly, snapping the sword back into its sheath and tucking the weapon and the logbook beneath his arm. Captain Morehouse needed to see this.

"Sir," John said darkly from across the cabin. They turned at once and picked their way across the room, slipping here and there on wads of sodden paper or stumbling over a rolling bottle or jug.

They stepped up beside John, who pointed wordlessly towards the captain's large bed. The sheets, all of them soaked through, were rumpled as though someone had just climbed out of them. Against the water-marked pillow lay a small child's doll. John touched Deveau's shoulder and pointed into the corner of the cabin. There was a sewing machine and scattered wooden toys.

"It looks as though Captain Briggs had his wife and kid on board," John said grimly.

"God help us," Deveau muttered, looking around the cabin. "Where are they?"

Mr Lewes stood and flicked on the lights. The children blinked in the sudden brightness, shocked to find themselves abruptly thrown from the deserted deck and back in the classroom.

"But that's crazy," Max burst out. "No one just vanishes into thin air! I reckon pirates got them."

"Maybe," Mr Lewes said with a mysterious smile. "When Oliver Deveau and his men went down into the hold, they found the Mary Celeste's cargo was all there, exactly as it should have been. Untouched by pirates."

"What was the cargo?" Freddie asked.

"A good question. The ship was carrying 1,701 barrels of alcohol. Not the kind you could drink," Mr Lewes added quickly, seeing the looks on their faces. "It was a special kind called denatured alcohol; you couldn't drink a drop without getting seriously ill. Too much of the stuff would kill you!

"Anyway," he continued, "as I said, the barrels were intact, although it turned out that a small number of them were empty, as though their contents had evaporated or leaked out. Deveau also found one of the Mary Celeste's pumps, used for pulling water out of the cargo hold, had been taken apart as though it had broken, and someone had tried to fix it. When they climbed down to inspect the barrels in the hold, they splashed into three and a half feet of cold Atlantic water, that's just over a metre to you kids."

"So, the ship was sinking," said Gwen with finality.

"Ah, but that's what was strange..."

"It's all strange!" Freddie interrupted and Mr Lewes simply gave an enigmatic smile again before continuing.

"Upon closer inspection, Deveau found that the Mary Celeste was almost completely shipshape. Aside from the tattered sails and a broken compass in the cabin, the ship was entirely seaworthy. There was a little water in the hold, yes, but she definitely wasn't sinking. So why then, was there no crew on board? Where had the captain and his family gone and why?"

Max got to his feet like an actor upon the stage and turned dramatically to face his classmates.

"I'll go first," he said confidently. "I know exactly what happened..."

2
MAX'S TALE

The Mary Celeste sat low in the Atlantic water. It was surrounded by a thick, white fog that floated just above the ocean's surface. The nearby islands, spotted the night before through the spyglass, were now hidden from sight behind the clouds.

Shivering in the cold, seaman Boz Lorensen stamped his feet against the deck as he watched the sunrise illuminating the fog to the east, setting it glowing like a bedside lamp. Boz was the youngest member of the crew and, as such, it was always he who had to take the night's watch. The coldest, most lonely watch of all. He found it almost impossible to keep himself awake during the long nights, silent but for the gentle lapping of the waves against the hull or the flapping of the sails above his head.

For nearly three weeks now the Mary Celeste had been at sea, the wind in her sails blowing her eastwards across the Atlantic and towards her destination in Italy. It had been eighteen nights of long, lonely watches for Boz. Yet something this morning felt different. Perhaps it was the suffocating fog that kept even the endless ocean from sight. Perhaps it was one too many nights of big waves and stormy winds. Boz stood at the rail, squinted out into the mist and saw nothing. It was like being engulfed in an endless cloud. Somewhere beneath his feet the rest of the crew were sleeping peacefully, enjoying their last minutes of rest before the sun woke them and set them about their work.

Just as Boz turned to walk his well-trodden path across the deck, he thought he saw a shadow moving through the fog beyond. He froze and stared into the whiteness, glowing yellow as the sun climbed ever higher somewhere beyond the haze. But he saw nothing. It must have been a sea bird, far from its home, diving amongst the swirling mist. As he was about to turn away, convinced the shadow had been nothing more than a figment of his own tired brain, he saw it again. The silhouette of the mast and sails of a tall ship, full of the breeze and moving steadily towards them. Boz squinted, trying to make out the ship's flag, anything that would identify the vessel, but in the weak morning light he could make out nothing but its vague outline.

Footsteps rang along the deck behind him, making him

jump out of his skin.

"You're jumpy this morning little brother! What's got you spooked?" Volkert joked. He was two years older than Boz, and two inches taller at that.

"I'm not spooked!" Boz snapped. "You made me jump is all."

Volkert stepped up beside his brother and looked out into the mist. "It's like we're stuck in the clouds, isn't it?" he said.

"I saw something," Boz said, pointing. "A ship."

Volkert peered into the fog for a moment before he too made out the sails bearing down on them. "I see it," Volkert said, suddenly serious.

"Shall I wake the captain?" Boz asked. For every night he'd spent alone watching, not once had he had reason to ring the bell or wake the captain. He had been beginning to think that this journey, an adventure he'd been looking forward to for years, would turn out to be the most boring month of his life.

"Not yet. Let's see what happens. They probably can't see us in this mist; they'll change course as soon as they do."

As the brothers watched, cold hands against the railings, the sails crept ever closer. Bit by bit the huge sheets of canvas emerged from the white fog.

"Do you see a flag?" Volkert asked. Boz started to shake his head, but then cried out suddenly as he saw a black flag rising up the centre mast. With jerking movements, the flag was hoisted into place at the very top of the ship, flapping in the morning breeze like an angry bird.

"A Jolly Roger!" Boz cried, panicked. "Pirates!"

Without saying a word, Volkert turned and grabbed the rope that hung beneath the large brass bell behind them. He pulled, pounding the metal and sending ringing shock waves like cannon blasts rolling across the silent deck.

"Boz, come here! Keep ringing until everyone is up!" Volkert bellowed, staring in terror at the wraith-like ship bearing down upon them, a demon bursting from the fog.

"Boz!" he shouted again over the ringing of the bell. The boy was startled from his horror and stumbled away from the rail, grabbing the rope from his brother and pounding it against the bell over and over again.

Volkert charged along the deck, leaping over folded sails, and crashing into a figure climbing out of the hatchway. Volkert didn't stop to say sorry but ran past and skidded to a halt outside the captain's cabin, hammering his fist against the door. He didn't wait for a reply, turning the handle and bursting into the room.

Captain Briggs, his hair combed back and his jacket, already buttoned despite the early hour, looked up startled from his desk. He held his pen steady over the ship's logbook, he'd barely finished writing the morning's date: 25th November 1872. As he stared at Volkert, drops of ink fell steadily against the polished wood of his desk.

"Captain, it's pirates!" Volkert gasped.

"What is it, Benjamin?" a woman's voice, softly spoken and heavy with sleep, came from the back of the room. Volkert looked over the captain's oiled hair and saw a woman in a white nightgown sitting up on the bed.

Beside her a small child lay, still sleeping, amongst the sheets and blankets.

"Pirates!" Volkert said again.

Mrs Briggs gave a cry of horror, a hand held against her mouth. Briggs threw down his pen and left the page empty and waiting. He turned to his wife.

"Sarah, get Sophia up and in her coat. Volkert, take them below deck - now!" As he spoke, Briggs snatched his belt, the buckles polished and shining, and wrapped it about his waist, fastening it as he marched out of his cabin.

"That's enough, Boz," Briggs barked as he stepped up alongside the pale boy still ringing the bell. Briggs pushed between the seamen gathered anxiously along the railing, six of them in all. He took the spyglass one of them offered and raised it in the direction they were all looking.

In the shuddering circle at the end of the glass, the black flag, emblazoned with a white skull, swam into view. He lowered the glass and looked darkly across at his first mate and best friend, Albert. Albert's moustache was quivering, his cheeks pale.

"The men are armed with whatever they could find. We'll be fish to the slaughter! Who knew pirates still sailed these waters?" he said.

Briggs looked along the line of his terrified crew. They weren't soldiers or warriors. They were merchant sailors, carrying cargo that was worthless to anyone but the buyer. Boz stood wringing his hands, while Arian was binding thick ropes around his fists, turning them into weapons. Young Gotleib was menacingly patting a boat hook against the palm of his hand, the angry metal glinting in

the sunlight. Heavy
and tall Edward,
larger than life in both size and
personality, had downed his cooking
tools below deck, all aside from two mean-
looking butcher's knives that he had thrust
into his belt. Farthest away was Andrew, the second
mate on the ship, his dark features turned even
blacker with fear and anger. He was the only one of
them who wasn't staring fixedly at the approaching
pirate ship; instead his eyes were lowered as he loaded
a long wooden pistol.

"What're you doing?" Briggs snapped, barging past his
crew and snatching the pistol from Andrew.

"We're not going to stand by and do nothing!" Andrew
snapped back. "This is all we have!"

"Exactly," said Briggs coldly, stuffing the pistol into
the back of his belt. "This is all we have! My wife and
child are on board this ship. I will not risk their lives
by starting a fight we cannot win. No, we're going to
bargain. These pirates will come abroad, they'll see we
have nothing of value and they will leave us unharmed."

Andrew scowled in disbelief, but he knew better than
to speak up against his captain's orders and he kept a
wise silence.

As the sun rose the clouds of fog finally began to lift,
wisps of mist drifting away on the breeze. As the still
water of the Atlantic came into view, so did the pirate
ship, close enough now for them to see the figurehead
of Medusa, her snarling face framed by snakes, at the
prow of the ship. On the deck they saw the pirates,
swarming over the railings, climbing down ladders into
little rowing boats. Three boats in total, each carrying

no fewer than ten men, lowered their oars into the water and began pulling towards the Mary Celeste and its terrified crew. In the first raft a pirate captain stood tall, a wide brimmed hat pulled low over their face and thick, curly red hair falling around their shoulders. The figure raised an arm and pointed towards the Mary Celeste, their prey. The captain stood with one knee raised, a carved wooden leg resting against the prow of the raft.

"Hold steady," Briggs warned his crew as they trembled on the deck, lifeless sails flapping gently above their heads. They pressed together. "No heroics from anyone; we can't fight these men. One ill-thought-out action and we'll wind up dead."

The sound of ladders clanking against their hull echoed across the deck and one by one pirates began swarming over the sides like ants. Dirty hands grabbed the rails, knives clenched between teeth. They leapt over the rails and landed on the deck. One after the other, outnumbering the Mary Celeste's crew four to one. They circled menacingly around the trembling sailors, snarling and jeering at them, laughter sparkling in their wicked eyes.

At last that wide hat and bushy red hair rose up and the pirate captain swung a carved wooden leg onto the deck with a clunk. At the sight of their leader the pirates stopped messing around and stood to attention, awaiting their orders.

The pirate captain looked up and the huddled crew saw the scarred face of a woman. Their cook, Edward, knives still gleaming at his belt, gave a cry of surprise at the sight of a female pirate. The captain tilted her head to the side and smirked at the crew, relishing their shock.

"I never get bored of the look on the faces of those I

capture," she said, walking along the line of crew and looking them up and down, her wooden leg clunking with every other step. "I am Captain Andromeda Blunt and this is my ocean you're passing through."

She raised her arm and gestured to the endless ocean surrounding them, not another soul for miles, no one to signal for help.

"Fishlegs, Basker, check the hold, let's see what booty this ol' Mary is carrying and what they can offer as payment for sailing so unwisely through my waters."

Two gnarly men, scarred and filthy, nodded and vanished down the hatchway. The remaining pirates drew together, closing the gap, leaving no room for the stricken crew to escape.

"Bind them," she ordered and at once the Mary Celeste crew found their hands pulled roughly together and bound tightly with rope. The smell of the pirates was terrible, as though they had never washed. The blood of their victims was caked in their hair and the remains of their dinner stuck between their teeth. As Edward was bound, the hunched pirate in front of him pulled the knives from the cook's belt and waggled them teasingly in front of his face before throwing them overboard with a splash.

Briggs alone remained free and, as Andromeda stepped up before him, two of her men seized him and pulled his hands tightly behind his back.

"Here, Captain," one of them said, pulling the loaded pistol from Briggs's belt and handing it to Andromeda.

She inspected the weapon with a smile, before tucking it behind the gleaming buckle of her own belt. "Not planning anything heroic I hope?" She didn't wait for an answer. "Take me to your cabin. Let's see what the Mary Celeste has to offer."

Briggs was marched across the deck, gnarly hands digging roughly into his shoulders, as the rhythmic footsteps of Andromeda Blunt echoed along behind him. The door to the captain's cabin was open, swinging gently in the breeze. As they moved into the darkness of the room, Andromeda looked around taking in the unmade bed, where the impression of a small child could still be seen amongst the blankets. She took in Sarah's sewing machine, an unfinished dress still draped across it, and she took in the toys scattered about the floor; alphabet blocks and a painted doll.

At that moment, a pirate burst around the door. "We found a woman and child hiding below deck Captain!" A cruel smile spread across Andromeda's face as she looked at Briggs.

"So, you brought your wife and child along for a family outing, did you?"

"Leave them alone!" Briggs shouted. "Take what you like but hurt no one! They're unarmed; they're harmless!"

Andromeda nodded slowly as he spoke, before turning to the pirate in the doorway. "And the cargo?"

"Useless, Captain. Barrels of alcohol, stinks like hell and no good for drinking. This ship's a bust."

Andromeda walked thoughtfully across to Briggs' desk. She ran her fingers along the unfinished entry of the ship's log, nothing but a date and location inked in. She picked up random items, a sextant, a gleaming compass, and tucked them into the pockets of her long leather coat. "If the cargo is of no value, then we shall have to get our money in other ways." she said at last. Behind her, Briggs breathed out a sigh of relief.

"Gather the crew into the boats; they should fetch us a pretty penny in ransom or sale."

The pirate in the doorway leered, showing off teeth both missing and blackened. "What of the woman and child?"

Andromeda appeared to think for a moment. "The family too," she said at last, and the pirate vanished from the doorway with a chuckle. "You two, gather up anything of value," she said.

The pirates holding Briggs released him, crossing to the desk and turning out the drawers, scattering the contents across the floor and pocketing anything of value.

Briggs stood rooted to the spot, his fists clenching and unclenching, as the pirates ransacked his cabin, as his family and his crew were even now being loaded into boats to be kidnapped and sold into slavery, or worse. He looked about the room for anything he could use as a weapon, his eyes falling at last upon the ceremonial sword mounted on the wall above his bed. A gift from his father that had proudly adorned the cabin wall of every ship he'd ever commanded. Without pausing to think it through, Briggs crossed the cabin, sending his daughter's toys scattering across the floor, and reached

31

up to grab the sword. As Andromeda realised what was happening, her pirates distractedly rummaging through the family's belongings, Briggs had already pulled the blade from its scabbard.

Briggs gave a cry of rage and leapt at Andromeda. They crashed into one another, falling back against the floor. Before Briggs had a chance to wield the sword Andromeda pulled Andrew's pistol from her belt and hit Briggs around the head with the butt. As the pistol went spinning across the floor, he staggered back, collapsing into the binnacle, the wooden cabinet that held the compass in place. As he fell to the ground amongst the shattered glass, the needle of the broken compass spinning wildly, Andromeda stepped up. With her wooden leg she pinned the skirt of Briggs' coat to the floor.

Slowly and deliberately, she bent down towards the stricken captain, her black eyes boring into his. "You have proved yourself more trouble than you are worth to me. Your cargo is useless and you're too reckless to keep around. Nobody needs a hero amongst their captives. No one pays for a hero."

As she spoke Briggs became aware of her arm moving beside him. There was a gentle scrape of metal against wood as Andromeda took up the dropped sword. As they stared into each other's eyes, one helpless, one leering with anger and disgust, a head poked through the door.

"Captain," it said in a gravelly voice, "the crew are loaded up; they're being taken to the Gorgon as we speak."

Andromeda turned her head slightly, the sword still gripped in her hand, her eyes still locked on Briggs.

"And the woman and child?"

"Awaiting your orders, Captain."

Andromeda looked back at Briggs thoughtfully. "Load them up in the lifeboat," she said darkly. "Set them adrift."

"No!" Briggs bellowed struggling to get up, pinned in place by her leg like a butterfly against a cork board.

In a burst of malice, Andromeda slashed furiously with the sword, and Captain Briggs knew no more.

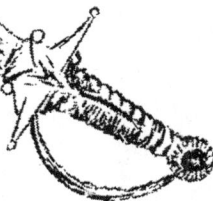

3
DON'T BE STUPID!

The classroom exploded into chatter as Max finished his dramatic tale.

"What a load of rubbish!" Alice cried, outraged.

"That was so cool," said Freddie enthusiastically, clapping Max on the shoulder to congratulate him. "Did Briggs really get killed?"

"Of course, he did!" said Max. "He was run through with his own sword for trying to be a hero!"

"What an awful ending for Sarah and Sophia," Alice said, folding her arms in disgust. "Just lost at sea like that. Luckily, it was a load of utter nonsense!"

"Says who?" Max snapped angrily.

Mr Lewes stepped in, raising his hands for silence. "That was certainly a thrilling and well-told tale, Max. I think it's safe to say you had us all a bit nervous!" He looked around at the club members, each of them still muttering darkly or, in Freddie's case, grinning with excitement. "I wonder, what was your evidence for this theory, Max?"

Max, still standing centre stage at the front of the room, took a deep breath and began. "There's so much evidence to support the pirate theory! They found actual blood stains on the sword for a start. Not to mention the scratches along the railings of the ship and the fact that the lifeboat was missing. Some of Briggs's equipment was also stolen from his desk..."

Alice and Gwen shouted protests, but Max raised his voice. "And the compass in the cabin was smashed and broken, exactly like I said!"

"Some good arguments there, Max." Mr Lewes turned to Alice. "You seem particularly upset with this version of events. How come?"

"You know Alice," Freddie said. "She doesn't like it when anything bad happens to anyone!"

"That's not a bad thing," said Mr Lewes, winking at Alice.

"It's nothing to do with that!" Alice snapped. "There's just no evidence."

"Ok, so let's hear your thoughts," Mr Lewes said. Alice stood up with a flourish and shooed Max aside.

"There's just no way pirates attacked the Mary Celeste," she began. "For a start, pirates didn't even exist anymore by 1872."

"But ..." Max interrupted, and Alice held up a hand to stall him.

"Also, the Mary Celeste had a cargo of alcohol, that would have had no value to pirates at all. They just wouldn't attack a ship like that, it would be a waste of their time - even if they had existed!"

Mr Lewes nodded. "Alice is right; pirates weren't that common by the time the Mary Celeste was at sea. The Golden Age of Piracy was a couple of centuries before the events we're talking about. However, pirates certainly did exist, even if they weren't very common."

"See!" Max said triumphantly.

"Fine," said Alice, unfazed. "But the whole sword thing is just silly. They never found any blood on the sword!"

"They did too!" Max said crossly.

Mr Lewes stepped in again to cool down the argument. "I'm sorry Max, but I'm afraid Alice is right on this one. The investigators did find a brown stain on the blade of the sword that had been in Captain Briggs' cabin. However, when they did some tests on it they discovered that the brown stains were actually rust and not blood. So the sword in his cabin had never been used to hurt another person, and certainly not to kill anyone!"

"Fine," said Max grumpily. "It was a good story though!"

"Oh, no doubt about that at all, Max! It was a very dramatic tale, and there were lots of people back then who thought that pirates could have been responsible for the crew's disappearance. It was very thoroughly looked in to by the investigators at the time, but they just couldn't find enough evidence to support the theory. Thank you for starting things off, Max, it's not easy going first! Who wants to go next?" He looked around at the Clueless Club.

"I'll go," Gwen said. She shrugged off her jacket and threw it over the back of her chair before moving to the front of the room. The club let out a gasp.

"Whoa!" Freddie said. "What happened to your hand?"

Without the long, trailing sleeves of her jacket they could see clearly that Gwen only had one hand. Her right arm simply ended at the wrist with little digits where fingers would have been.

Mr Lewes stood up to intervene, but Gwen reacted first looking down at her right arm in mock horror. "Oh man, I've lost it again!" she said sarcastically, pretending to search the floor around her.

"Seriously though," said Max, "what happened to your hand?"

"Oh this?" she said holding up her arm. "Shark attack; I was lucky to escape with my life."

Freddie and Max stared, their mouths hanging open. Alice, however, chuckled and smirked as though she knew something the boys didn't. Ignoring the boys, who were throwing covert glances at Gwen in the hopes of seeing the terrifying scars they imagined a shark might leave, Alice gave her an encouraging nod and a thumbs up.

Mr Lewes changed the subject. "So, Gwen, what do you think happened to the crew of the Mary Celeste? If pirates didn't kidnap them, what did happen?"

Gwen paused for a moment, as if steeling herself for their reaction, before saying: "I think the crew of the Mary Celeste were abducted by aliens."

4
GWEN'S TALE

Eddie Head was always up before the sun. At 23 years old he was one of the younger members of the crew, but his six years at sea as a cook had taught him that sailors were hungry when they woke up, and that hungry sailors were grumpy sailors. His body would wake itself without fail, always half an hour before dawn.

The morning of the 25th November 1872 was no different. He rolled out of his hammock, leaving his crewmates snoring and rocking gently around him. After stretching out his cold muscles, he moved into the dingy, narrow galley, the hanging pots and pans above his head clinking gently against one another as the ship rocked. He could barely see anything but Eddie could make his way around the galley blindfolded. He reached out for a grimy cloth and used it to grab the handle of the stove, twisting it open with a clank. With the poker that hung above he reached into the glowing embers and stoked them to life, chucking in a handful of fresh coal from the bucket beside him. Slamming the door shut - there was a sleepy grunt from one of the sailors - he lifted the lid from the kettle that sat atop the stove. The water inside wasn't boiling but light wisps of steam rolled up from its surface. He lifted down a mug from the hooks behind him and threw a handful of ground coffee beans into the bottom, before lifting the kettle with the cloth and filling it to the brim. Setting the kettle back atop the stove, he gave the mug a quick stir and lifted it in both hands. Savouring the warmth, he made his way between the rows of swinging hammocks, where his crewmates were beginning to stir.

He climbed the steep staircase, threw open the hatch and stepped up onto the deck. The cold ocean air hit him like a wave, and he shivered as he kicked the hatch shut behind him. Steam was billowing from the mug in his hands, swirling up into the cloudy mist that surrounded the deck. There was a strange metallic taste in the air and something unexplainable made the hair on the back of his neck prickle and stick up.

"Boz?" he called out, a slight shake to his voice. He was relieved to hear the answering call from high above him. The ship's watch, a man the same age as Eddie but half his size, came clambering down the rigging like a monkey.

"Cheers, Eddie," he said, his English perfect despite

a heavy German accent. Boz took the mug and blew away the steam before taking a grateful sip.

"Cold night, eh?" Eddie said, peering out into the darkness. Somewhere through the mist, far out of sight, a light was starting to rise and set the fog aglow. Eddie shivered and wrapped his arms around himself. As Boz slurped noisily at his coffee, the two men watched the growing light from the deck of the Mary Celeste, silent except for the occasional flap of a sail or slap of a rope against the mast.

"You see that?" Boz said, lowering his mug and moving closer to the railing.

"It's just the sunrise," Eddie said.

"Never seen no green sunrise before," Boz said.

And he was right, of course. Even as Eddie stared, he could see the glowing light, that he had assumed was nothing more than the sun rising beyond the horizon, was actually glowing a vivid, unnatural green. Whatever the source of the light, it set the endless clouds of mist that hung over the Atlantic on fire in bright, leafy shades. Without thinking the two men backed away from the light. As they moved a sudden noise rose up from the mist, a kind of buzzing hum that grew louder and louder, working its way into their very bones.

"It's coming closer!" Boz shouted in a panic, stumbling over some coiled ropes on the deck and sending his mug smashing to the ground. Sure enough, as the two men stumbled back, a shadow passed through the mist silhouetted by the blinding green light. A long flat shape buzzed towards them. As it drew close to the ship the shadow, whatever it was, suddenly pulled up. With a metallic wail it swooped upwards, sending the mist spiralling into tiny tornadoes all around them

41

before it vanished. Eddie heaved Boz to his feet.

"What the devil was that?" he asked, his breathing ragged and his heart racing.

"I don't know," Boz panted, clinging to Eddie's arm. "But I think it's gone..."

Crouching low the pair looked upwards, beyond the flapping sails, and into the clouds of fog above them. White fog, tinged with the pale yellow of a nice, normal sunrise. Whatever the strange green light had been, whatever that flying shadow, it seemed to have vanished as soon as it had come. They turned on the spot, looking all around them.

It was Eddie who broke the silence, with a nervous laugh. "What fools," he said, with a forced chuckle, his heart still pounding.

Boz looked at him, his face white as the mist that hung over the water. "You think we imagined that?" he asked.

Eddie raised his arms to gesture around them. "I don't see anything now, do you? I reckon we need to get ourselves some more sleep, am I right?" He grinned as convincingly as he could and slapped Boz on the shoulder.

"But," Boz began, rubbing his shoulder absently, "we should at least tell the captain..."

"Nah! Do me a favour," Eddie said, pulling Boz close. "Don't tell a soul. We'll be the butt of their jokes for the rest of the trip. Let's just keep this, not that it even happened, between us, ok?"

Boz nodded slowly.

"Good man!" Eddie boomed, patting him on the

shoulder again. "Now, I'd better get cracking with breakfast. Got me some hungry mouths to feed. And you, get yourself some rest, ok?" With that, without waiting for a reply, Eddie turned his back on the boy, on the plain, traditional sunrise, and descended back through the hatchway into the darkness and the safety below deck. As he weaved between the hammocks his crewmates were finally getting up.

Volkert, sitting on his hammock and rubbing his beard as if trying to wake himself up, called; "Oi, Eddie. What was all that hollering about? Has my baby brother spooked himself again?"

Eddie laughed harder than he normally would, a great forceful boom.

"Yeah, right. Kid's having nightmares again. We really ought to give him a break from the night watch!" He gave a gruff laugh.

Keeping his face turned away, Eddie scooted past the first mate, Albert, who was leaning over a barrel and splashing water on his face. He tipped his cap to his best friend Arian, as the man rummaged in his hammock for his pipe, before diving back into the security of his warm, familiar galley.

The sun was rising above deck, and Eddie was grateful for the light. He tried to block out the memory of what they had just seen. The green light, the strange thrumming noise, the prickling sensation at the back of his neck, the metallic taste in his mouth. He focused on his tasks, on checking the stove and preparing the breakfast meal for the crew. He focused on the comforting creaks of the ship, on the grumbling of the sleepy men behind him, readying themselves for another long day at sea.

He grabbed a loaf of bread from a cupboard, it was solid, heavy and felt like a brick inside its waxed wrapping. He unwrapped it quickly, trying to pin his attention on the crackling of the waxed paper, on the feel of the knife in his hand. He tried not to think of that sound, that light. He readied the knife against the hard crust of the loaf and took a deep, steadying breath. He could swear that he could still hear that awful metallic whine, that he could still see the eerie green glow. He stood still, breathing deeply and trying to rid his mind of the experience above deck. But with every breath he took, the humming buzz seemed to get louder, not quieter. The green glow seemed to grow brighter, not dimmer.

As Eddie stood, desperately trying to breathe himself back to calm, he became aware that the ship had fallen silent around him. The hairs on the back of his neck and along his arms began to prickle again. Slowly, the knife in his hand shaking now, Eddie opened his eyes and peered around the side of the stove and towards the hammocks. He could see every detail clearly, illuminated as they were in an eerie, bright green light. The light seemed to be sliding across the deck of the ship above, casting shadows that rolled over the faces of his crewmates. As Eddie stared, his ears ringing and panic rising, he watched their motionless shadows slide across the floor as the green light passed overhead. The men weren't moving, not so much as a blink or a breath. Albert was still hunched over the barrel, his hands frozen in front of his face, droplets of cold water dripping from his fingers. Volkert was suspended, one foot on the ground, the other still raised high, as if he had been turned to stone just as he was jumping down from his hammock.

In a daze, Eddie left the safety of the galley, knife in hand

and loaf forgotten, as he drifted towards his crewmates, the men with whom he'd spent every waking hour since leaving Nova Scotia weeks before. There was Gotlieb, one leg into his trousers, the other holding him up like a flamingo, as still as though he had been carved from wood. There was Andrew, white shaving foam frothing around his chin like a beard, the blade raised to sweep through the bubbles. Arian, one arm slung casually over his hammock holding a pipe and the other hand raised to pull some ashes and old tobacco from the bowl.

"Arian?" Eddie said quietly, his voice trembling. He reached out with a shaking finger and tapped his friend's arm. Nothing. Not so much as a hint of a snigger or a smirk. All the while that green light pulsed above deck, that buzzing whined constantly in his ears.

That was it: this was all some kind of stupid prank. "It's not funny," Eddie said, his voice rising now. He raised a hand ready to cuff Arian around the back of the head and just as he was about to bring down the blow, a scream from above deck cut across the buzz. Eddie didn't stop to think about what he was doing; he recognised that voice. Boz was somewhere above him and he was screaming for his life. Eddie dropped the knife, it landed point-down in the wooden boards, and took two steps at a time as he rushed up onto deck.

At least he had thought he was going on deck, but this was not the Mary Celeste as he had known it. And he'd known every rivet, every plank, as though they were parts of his own body. The air around the deck was crystal clear, he could see everything, every rope, every splinter, in vivid detail, but beyond the railings there was a wall of white cloud. He could see nothing beyond the deck of the ship. He turned his head upwards where the thrumming noise and that green glow seemed to be coming from, shining down on the Mary Celeste like a spotlight. He saw the ship's white sails, floating eerily upwards as though they were being sucked towards the light. He could see Boz, the man he'd been speaking to mere moments ago, high up amongst the flapping sails. But he wasn't holding on to the rigging, he was floating like a leaf on the wind, his arms flailing wildly as he screamed. Boz rolled over as he cried out, his feet dragged upwards towards the light, his head pointing down towards the deck. He saw Eddie as he flailed.

"Eddie!" he screamed. "Help me!" But Eddie stood frozen to the spot, watching his friend rising ever higher into the light until he could see no more, blinded by a green light, so bright it was like staring at the sun. Boz's screams vanished a second after his body and Eddie was left staring blindly up among the flapping sails, the loose ropes of the rigging dancing like snakes.

He had no idea how long he stood there, his eyes unseeing, his brain barely able to cope with the strange turn his morning had so suddenly taken. A creaking noise cut through the strange hum and Eddie's wide eyes dropped down to the deck where he saw the door to Captain Briggs' cabin opening outwards. The tight knot in his stomach loosened with relief - Captain

Briggs was coming! He would know what to do. Eddie might have gone mad, the crew like statues, Boz vanishing into the light, but Briggs would set it all straight. Maybe he did need a lie down after all; and there he was telling Boz to get some more sleep! Eddie could have laughed with relief as he saw the captain's smart buttoned jacket appear in the doorway.

"Captain!" Eddie cried, stumbling towards the door. Then he stopped, drawing up short beneath the spotlight. He could feel his hair drifting around his ears as though he was caught in a strong wind. Briggs was indeed coming out of the cabin, but he wasn't walking.

The captain, his hair not yet groomed for the day, his buttons only half fastened, was drifting like a doll through the door. His head bumped lightly against the doorframe as he began to rise into the sky. He was followed at once by a tiny child, her white nightshirt rippling in the invisible breeze. The girl's eyes were closed and she was curled up as though she'd been lifted, fast asleep from her bed. A third figure emerged, following her husband and daughter into the green sky above the deck. Sarah Briggs' skirts were fanning about her like a parachute, her eyes were open, but her face was expressionless and calm, as though she was simply out for a stroll. One by one the Briggs family rose, a corner of the wildly flapping sail beating against Sarah's skirts, until each of them vanished into the centre of the light.

Eddie let out a noise, somewhere between a scream and a groan. Unable to bear being alone on this eerie, desolate deck for a second longer he ran towards the open hatchway. He was going to wake up the crew, by any means possible, and if that were to fail at least he

47

could hide in the safety of his warm, familiar galley. He was brought to a sudden halt as the face of his best friend drifted upwards out of the hatch. As Arian's shoulders and arms followed, rising upwards like a kite, Eddie saw the pipe still held frozen in his hands, his arm sticking out awkwardly to the side where he'd been slouching against his hammock.

Eddie backed away from the hatch and stared as his friend rose silently into the sky, drifting up through the canopy of sails until he too vanished into that impossible green light, into the wind that blew even though he knew it shouldn't. Behind Arian came blobs of a strange white froth, out of place until Eddie saw Albert, his face still covered in shaving foam, come floating up into the sky.

Eddie felt something behind him then. He couldn't have said what it was; it wasn't a noise, it wasn't a touch, it was simply a feeling that his isolation had ended, a feeling that there was someone else onboard the Mary Celeste. Slowly, unwillingly, Eddie turned around. Standing at the prow of the ship, staggered like bowling pins, were three figures. They wore no clothes, yet somehow were not naked. They had no shape, yet were somehow human. No colour, yet somehow grey. Eddie's panic had reached such a level that, like the brightest centre of the green light above, it could almost not be felt. He was numb, imprisoned within his terror.

"What do you want?" he stammered, his voice whipped away instantly by the wind that did not blow. The figures had no mouths, they could not speak, and yet he heard their words in his head as though they had knocked on his skull and simply walked in.

Be calm. The words said. *We do not wish to harm you.*

48

We are the curious.

"Why are you here?" Eddie asked.

We are here to learn. The figure at the front tilted its head to the side as if to say, 'what a silly question!'

"But why are you here? Why the Mary Celeste?" Eddie's eyes drew up as the shadow of the first mate, his boss, hands still cupped in front of his unwashed face, drifted across him.

You are alone here. Your disappearance is not seen. No one will know we were here.

"Oh they'll know alright!" Eddie shouted. His voice strengthened by his rage. "The whole world will know. You won't get away with this!" He scrabbled at his belt, where usually a kitchen knife or two were stashed, but all he felt was the cold canvas of his once-white apron. The knife, he remembered with a rising sense of doom, was below deck, stuck in the floorboard beneath Arian's empty hammock. He knew then that all he could do was run. The hatchway behind him was not an option, as the last members of his crew still drifted slowly and unhurriedly into the sky.

He dived around the side of the hatch and ran to the open doorway of Briggs' cabin. Never before had he entered the captain's private chambers, but Briggs was long gone now, out of reach and sight. Eddie crashed into the room, slamming the door shut behind him. As he staggered across the floor, blindly kicking toys aside as he went, a shaft of green light suddenly cut across the floor, casting his startled shadow across the unmade bed. He didn't need to turn, he could feel the figures behind him, he could sense them standing in that same strange formation in the doorway, opened without a sound.

It is time for you to come, the words said. *The others are waiting for you.*

"No! You won't take me too!" Eddie thought he was shouting, but his ears heard nothing. As he cried out he felt a pull against his leg. He could feel no hands gripping him, no pressure against his trousers, but he was pulled all the same, backwards towards the doorway, towards the figures and the light.

"No!" he screamed again, leaping forwards and lunging for the only thing he could reach, the wooden binnacle that held the compass in place. He wrapped his arms around the wooden post as though it was a tree trunk, fighting with everything he had against the force that wanted to drag him into nothingness. A shadow fell over him, blocking out the light, and then the figures were there, standing around him, watching his plight.

Your effort is wasted. We are the curious; we leave no one behind.

"Not me!" As Eddie bellowed, fear and rage engulfing him, the binnacle started to creak and splinter, unable to hold him against the mysterious force that gripped him. The wood snapped and bent, the glass case that held the compass smashing against the floor as Eddie was dragged across the planks, screaming, into the air and vanished into the green, whirring light.

The Mary Celeste sat low in the Atlantic water. As the morning of the 25th November 1872 finally

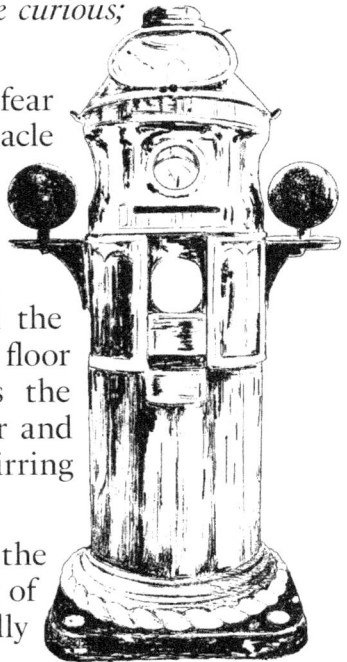

50

dawned with a pale, orange glow, the sea mist that had lingered in the hours before dawn melted away, leaving the ship drifting in the crystal-clear ocean. The sails hung ragged against the rigging, as though they'd fought recently through a storm. The Mary Celeste sat low in the Atlantic water, drifting silently into nothingness.

5
NO PROOF

The classroom was as silent as the Mary Celeste as everyone stared at Gwen. She shuffled her feet a little nervously, until the room erupted and everyone started talking at once.

"Wow!" cried Max.

"That - was - epic!" added Freddie.

"Erm... what on earth?" said Alice.

"Well, not on earth surely! You mean 'what in space', right?" said Freddie.

"Ha ha," Alice said sarcastically.

"Goodness me, Gwen," said Mr Lewes, "that was quite a story. It certainly gave me chills!"

Gwen grinned and gave a little bow as Mr Lewes led the clapping.

"So, where do we begin trying to unpick that tale?" he said.

"Well, it's not true!" Alice said decisively, with an apologetic smile as Gwen sat down.

"How do you know?" said Max. "The truth is they never found any one of the crew; they might well have been abducted by aliens. It happens all the time!"

"Does it indeed?" said Mr Lewes. "In all seriousness now, why can't the alien abduction be true, Alice?"

"Well, it's not that it can't be true. I don't think we can ever prove that aliens *weren't* there that day." She ignored Freddie as he punched the air excitedly. "The lifeboat was missing from the deck, for a start. How does the alien theory explain that?"

"Maybe Edward tried to escape using the lifeboat?" suggested Max.

"Or maybe it was swept overboard while the ship was drifting without any crew," said Gwen.

"I guess the trouble with the alien theory," Mr Lewes continued, "is that, as Alice said, it's almost impossible to prove that it didn't happen. There is no clear evidence that aliens were ever onboard the ship, but on the flip side there is no clear evidence to say that they definitely weren't. We simply don't know enough about alien life to know what they would or wouldn't have done."

Alice nodded, a little smugly.

"The key," Mr Lewes went on, "is whether or not you believe alien life exists, and if it did, whether it would spend its time abducting families from the middle of the Atlantic. Mysteries like this, where people vanish and there is no one left to tell the tale, often attract people who believe in alien abductions."

"So, how can we ever know, one way or another?" asked Max, frowning.

"Well, we can't," said Alice. "We can't possibly ever know, unless we find the aliens and ask them!"

"There really is only one way to discount the alien theory and that is to find a better, more believable theory as to what happened," Mr Lewes said.

Freddie stood up with a grin. "It sounds like it's my turn then, doesn't it?" he said as he moved to the front of the classroom, ready to tell his tale.

6

FREDDIE'S TALE

"**A**lright lads, out of bed you lazy lot!" Albert marched between the row of hammocks shaking the crew awake. In the galley, Edward, the ship's cook was clanking away, firing up the stove and getting the day's breakfast in order. As first mate aboard the Mary Celeste and second in command to the captain, Albert was responsible for getting everyone up and ready to face another long day at sea.

There was a loud grunting snore from one of the hammocks as he passed. Albert had been at sea for years, and a good chunk of those had been spent as second in command. He wasn't about to take any flak from the crew now. As the others looked on through sleepy eyes, Albert stopped alongside the snoring hammock.

"Oh I don't think so, Volkert!" he said and, with one swift motion, he flipped over the sleeping man's hammock, tipping him out onto the floor. Volkert gave a cry of shock and leapt to his feet in a rage, but as soon as he saw the first mate, he stood to attention and mumbled his apology.

"Don't ever make me ask twice," Albert said, patting Volkert's bright red cheek as the rest of the crew laughed uproariously. As he turned to walk away, the floorboards beneath his feet shuddered. The jolting movement sent the sailors staggering, tumbling back against the wall, tripping over chests and clinging onto their hammocks, still warm from the night. Albert gripped on to the wall and listened to the rumbling, grating sound that rocked the ship.

"What the devil was that?" Edward called, as he staggered out of the galley.

"Felt like an earthquake," said Volkert.

"You fool, we're in the middle of the Atlantic!" Arian replied.

"It felt like we hit something, or something dragged along the side of the ship," Albert said quietly.

Each of them stood motionless, waiting to see if it would happen again, but all was still, all was normal.

"Get yourselves ready and on deck, business as usual lads. I'll tell the captain." Albert said, turning away and pulling himself up the steep steps, two at a time, onto the deck.

In the early morning light, everything looked normal. A light sea mist still hung around the ship, but aside from that the ocean was as calm as glass, not so much as a ripple on the surface. Against the opposite railing a woman stood in a white dress, she held a small toddler in her arms and together they were peering over into the depths below. The youngest member of the crew, Boz, was walking towards him rubbing his eyes after a long and cold night shift.

"Did you see anything just now?" Albert asked him.

"That shudder do you mean? I saw nothing. I was up the rigging as well; it was like glass out there."

Albert nodded and gave Boz a clap on the shoulder before sending him below deck for some rest. Albert turned his back and rapped against the captain's cabin door.

"Enter!"

Inside the cabin was dimly lit, the burning lanterns swamped by the growing sunlight from outside. Toys littered the floor, and across the far side of the room Albert noticed the large bed, the sheets still rumpled from where the captain's young daughter had slept. Briggs was sat at his desk, the neck of his shirt still unfastened. He held a pen over the ship's logbook, he had written the date, 25th November 1872, but had yet to add anything else.

"What was that Albert?" Briggs leaned back in his chair and looked at his first mate. "Did I feel a shudder back there?"

"You did, Captain. We're six miles from shore so it can't have been a sandbank, and Boz reported a calm sea. Maybe driftwood, or a whale carcass?"

Briggs twiddled the pen between his fingers thoughtfully.

"We've certainly seen stranger things at sea," he said. "Conduct a thorough inspection all the same; check for any damage."

Albert nodded and backed out of the cabin, but before he could shut the door there was a sudden cry from the deck behind him. He couldn't make out the words, but the panicked tone was clear. Albert leapt back as Briggs rushed past him. He shielded his eyes from the rising sun and squinted up into the rigging where he could see the dark figure of Boz.

The boy was frantically pointing down at the surface of the water. Briggs and Albert ran to the railing and looked over into the depths. The water all around them had gone a strange shade of blue, almost black, as though the Mary Celeste was sailing in the midst of a giant ink spill.

"What the ...?" Briggs murmured, crossing to the other side of the ship, and seeing the same there.

"Oil slick?" Albert said. "Maybe we hit a barrel."

The slick stretched in a wide circle around the ship.

As they watched, a fish burst out of the water apparently gulping in mouthfuls of the strange bluey black water. No sooner had it appeared than another fish arose, followed by another. Before long the entire surface of the ocean was heaving and jumping with hundreds of thousands of fish. The animals, all rolling around the surface, were bashing into one another in a violent feeding frenzy.

"Looks like it's boiling," someone murmured behind Albert and he turned to see the rest of the crew, gathered nervously behind him. Their faces pale, their teeth clenched.

"The sound down there is deafening," Volkert said, gesturing towards the hatchway below deck. "Must be all those fish hitting the hull. What on earth are they doing?"

"It looks like they're feeding," Albert replied, a frown creasing his brown.

"Did you ever see anything like that before?" Edward asked. "I sure haven't."

Silently the crew shook their heads, staring at the unfamiliar ocean, boiling and teeming with fish. They were jolted out of their reverie by a cry behind them, the shout cut short by a loud splash.

"Man overboard! Port side!"

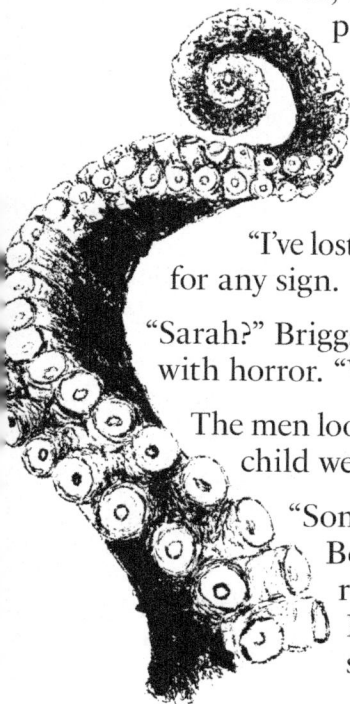

Boz, still hanging from the rigging, was pointing at the water on the opposite side.

"Who went over?" Albert shouted as the crew ran to the opposite railing and leant over to see.

"I've lost them!" Boz cried, squinting around for any sign.

"Sarah?" Briggs said suddenly, his voice cracking with horror. "Where are Sarah and Sophia?"

The men looked around, the captain's wife and child were nowhere to be seen.

"Something pulled them overboard!" Boz shouted, scrambling down the ropes and jumping onto the deck. Briggs grabbed the boy by the shoulders and shook him roughly.

59

"What was it? What pulled them over?!"

Boz shook his head and stammered. He'd not seen what it was; one moment the woman and her child were there, watching the fish over the railing, the next they were gone, dragged over into the churning water.

"Launch the lifeboat," Briggs ordered, his face a sheet of panic.

At once the stunned crew leapt into action, unstrapped the single lifeboat from its position on the deck and dragged it along its rails to the side of the ship. They were preparing to lower it, when something burst out of the water, sending fish spinning through the air and covering the deck in a splattering of inky salt water. The men let the lifeboat fall and, as it crashed against the surface of the water, they staggered back and stared up at the two vast tentacles that rose up into the sky like trees.

"Kraken!" someone bellowed; a sailor's worst nightmare.

As fat droplets of black water fell like rain, the crew could see suckers the size of dinner plates, pulsing and stretching, each of them rimmed with a ring of blade-like teeth. The tentacles reached towards the sky before, as one, they crashed down towards the deck. The crew scattered, diving and fleeing in all directions.

The tentacles moved like snakes, as though they had minds all of their own and were not simply the limbs of some horrific larger monster. They wormed their way across the deck; their suckers feeling and sensing motion, drawn towards the flailing crew.

Boz had made it to the hatchway before one of the tentacles wrapped itself around his leg. He gave a cry of shock and pain, before he was dragged with sickening

speed over the
side of the ship and
down into the murky,
boiling depths.

"Boz!" Volkert screamed. He grabbed the
rail and was about to dive in after his brother
when the second tentacle saved him the
job. It wound around his middle and
lifted him up into the air before it too
plunged down beneath the surface,
taking Volkert with it.

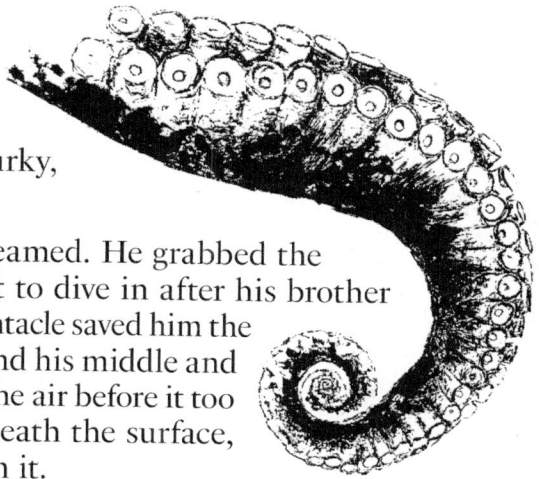

Andrew and Arian were the next to go, both of them
seized from behind as more tentacles burst from the
ocean, scattering ink and fish across the deck. As their
screams were cut short by the water, Gotleib staggered
across the deck and began frantically climbing the
rigging, desperate to put as much distance between
himself and those tentacles as possible, for all the good
it did him. The long, snake-like limbs, suckers throbbing
and teeth gleaming, rose higher than any mast could
and Gotleib was plucked down like a fruit from a tree.

Albert had fallen and lay, trembling, between folded
canvas sails. He watched, stunned, as the ship tilted and
rolled, little streams of inky sea water running between
the planks and back over the side into the hellish ocean
below. He watched numbly as Briggs, and the burly cook
Edward, stood with their backs against the wall of the
captain's cabin. They had armed themselves, Edward
with a gleaming carving knife in one hand and a heavy
iron skillet in the other, Briggs with a ceremonial sword
he'd seized from the wall of his cabin. The tentacles,
more now than Albert could count, were snaking their
way up the side of the hull, working into the hatches
and smashing out the windows. Two of them slithered

their way across the deck towards
the two seamen. With a battle
cry, Edward lunged forward
slashing at the tentacle with
his knife and beating at it with
the pan. The tentacle flinched,
thick, black blood oozing from
a gaping wound along its side.

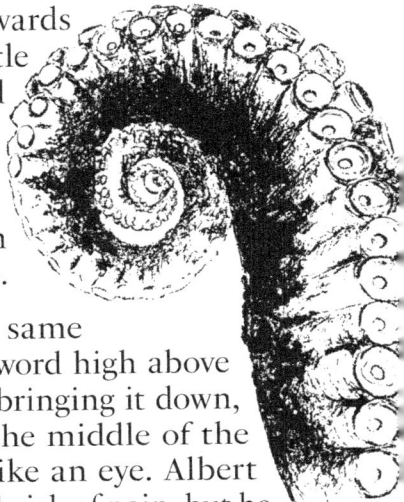

Briggs leapt forward at the same
moment, raising the small sword high above
his head in both hands and bringing it down,
stabbing straight through the middle of the
tentacle, piercing a sucker like an eye. Albert
could have sworn he heard a shriek of pain, but he
knew it was impossible, as the vile tentacles had no
mouths with which to cry out. But even as he thought it
he knew, with a sinking in his stomach, that somewhere
beneath them now, lurking in the blackness of the spill,
was the body to which these tentacles belonged. If the
tales were to be believed, it was a head of unimaginable
size, with razor-sharp teeth as long as a man is tall.
Hundreds upon hundreds of them, arrayed around the
opening to a putrid, death-filled stomach.

The Kraken was angry, its blood spilling across the
deck. More tentacles swarmed towards their attackers.
Edward and Briggs were lost amidst the tangle of slick,
wet muscles and Albert never saw them again. Instead,
he saw the mass of tentacles, tangled like a bramble bush
left to run wild, slowly seizing hold of the Mary Celeste
herself. They were squeezing down and he could hear
the snapping of the wood and feel the planks begin to
splinter. He was alone. He could hear no more screams,
no more furious and fearful cries. All he could hear was
the slow crushing of the ship, his home, beneath him

and the flapping and splashing of the countless fish that still bustled and fought in the waters around him.

From the corner of his eye, he saw a shape drift past, buffeted this way and that on the turbulent ocean - the lifeboat! In that moment he felt a swooping in his belly, a swelling of something, not relief as such, but maybe just a tiny bit of hope. He didn't stop to think it through; he didn't stop to look at the tentacles that slowly suffocated the Mary Celeste and everything within it. He hauled himself to his feet and he dived, his arms above his head, straight into the nightmare ocean beneath him. As the stinking mass of fish beat against his body and the putrid water filled his mouth he swam, arm over arm, towards the lifeboat as it drifted at the edge of the inky black spill. His body tingled all over as he dragged himself over the side and collapsed into the bottom of the tiny boat, the thrashing fish had left his skin red and smarting. Slowly, he pulled himself up and turned to look behind him at the Mary Celeste.

She was caught in a web of tentacles and was being pushed up out of the water. The suckers caressed the barnacles that covered her hull; the water poured down as though she were a sponge, wrung for every droplet. He could hear the splintering and the creaks as the Kraken slowly, inexorably, crushed the ship.

Barely aware of his chattering teeth and his shaking limbs, Albert took up the oars and struggled to clip them into place. He set one in with difficulty, his hands barely under control, before turning his attention to the other one. He kept his head down, trying his best to ignore the intense pounding of his heart and the shadow of the Mary Celeste, hanging above the surface of the ocean in a web of thorny tentacles, the life slowly being crushed out of her, splinter by splinter.

As he fumbled, the second oar slipped through his fingers, wet with inky black water, and fell into the ocean with a splash. He froze, his lifeboat had drifted beyond the thrashing school of hungry fish and the oar landed with a slap against the eerily calm surface of the Atlantic. Slowly he looked up. Was it his imagination or had the writhing tentacles holding the Mary Celeste also hesitated? Had they stopped, as if listening, as if they had heard the sound of an oar, clumsily dropped into the ocean.

As he stared, one by one the tentacles began to retreat back into the water, retreating backwards across the deck and unwinding themselves from the rigging, until the Mary Celeste fell back against the surface with a splash. She bobbed there, her sails dishevelled, her sides scratched, her decks waterlogged, but still she floated limply in the water.

There was a deathly calm all around him. No fish, no murderous tentacles, it was just Albert floating some distance away from the ship he'd once called home. He looked around him, turning in the boat, but as if nothing had happened at all, the Atlantic was once again as still and as calm as glass.

Slowly, Albert peered over the edge of the lifeboat and reached out a trembling hand towards the oar that floated there. It was just out of his reach. But with each moment of silence that passed, his racing heart seemed to calm a little and he dared to hope that his nightmare might finally have ended. He clung to the edge of the raft and stretched out, fumbling with his fingers and trying to snare the oar, to drag it back within his reach. As his fingertips made contact with the rough surface of the oar, a bubble rose up from the depths and popped beside him, leaving a black inky stain.

As he stared at the dark ripples, a larger bubble rose, pushing the oar further out of his reach as it popped, spreading the oily blackness until it swelled around him and engulfed the raft entirely. Slowly, his blood freezing in his veins, Albert pulled back his arm and sank to the floor of the life raft. He curled himself up beneath the bench and hugged his knees to his chest as he began to hear the fluttering and slapping of hundreds of fish against the flimsy hull. He knew now what would come next. He knew the Kraken, even now, was rising up beneath him like a demon from hell. Albert, first mate of the Mary Celeste, closed his eyes and prayed the end would come quickly.

7
IT CAN'T BE SO

"So.... what happened to Albert?" Gwen asked as the room fell into silence at the end of Freddie's tale. "Did he die?"

"Well, he was never found..." said Freddie, mysteriously.

Alice gave a shudder. "Poor man, I hope it was over quickly. That would have been terrifying!"

Gwen nodded in agreement. "I can't think of anything worse than being eaten alive by a giant octopus thing!"

"Certainly not a nice way to go," Mr Lewes agreed gravely. "Indeed, tales of the Kraken have been terrifying sailors for centuries. Even the Vikings feared the Kraken!"

"What was all that black water and the fish about?" Max asked.

"Well," Freddie said, glad somebody had asked. "Apparently, the Kraken would belch out all this nasty rotten liquid while it was lying at the bottom of the ocean. The gunk would float to the surface and hundreds of fish would swarm around it trying to eat all the rotten stuff from its gut. Then the Kraken would swoop up and feast on whatever it found at the top!"

"Yikes! Poor Albert!" said Max, giving a shudder at the thought of it.

"So, what do we think?" Mr Lewes asked. "Could Freddie's tale explain the disappearance of the crew of the Mary Celeste?"

"I don't think so," said Alice.

"You disagree with everything!" Freddie said indignantly. "Why couldn't the Kraken have taken the crew?"

"Well for a start you said that it was crushing the ship, there was no damage like that found on the ship at all!"

"Yeah," Gwen piped up. "Apart from the water below deck and some tatty sails, there was no real damage on the ship."

"And I guess if the Kraken really did have teeth all over its tentacles, then there would have been scratches all over the ship. Someone would have noticed," said Max, reluctantly. "I want it to be true; the Kraken is awesome! But there are so many problems with it; like how did Briggs' sword make its way back onto the wall of his cabin if he was holding it when he was swallowed by the beast?"

67

Freddie raised his hands as if in surrender. "Alright, alright," he said.

"It looks like you've been unanimously voted down, Freddie," Mr Lewes said. "The others are right, there really is no evidence anything as violent or destructive as a Kraken attack ever happened to the Mary Celeste. And of course, Max makes a good point about the sword being found back on the wall by the Dei Gratia crew!"

Mr Lewes smiled kindly at Freddie before he continued. "But I think we all agree that it was a superb and exciting tale! I won't lie; the Kraken is definitely very cool!" He turned to Alice.

"And so, that brings us to our final theory. You've been quite vocal about dismissing the others' stories, so I'm keen to hear what you've got in store for us!"

Freddie grinned, not looking remotely bothered, and took a little bow at the front of the room before stepping aside to allow Alice to take the floor. Freddie dropped back into his seat as the Clueless Club prepared themselves for the next tragic chapter in the story of the Mary Celeste.

8
ALICE'S TALE

The crew of the cargo ship, the Mary Celeste, was tired. They had been on duty for what felt like days, as the Atlantic Ocean rolled in the stormy weather. Clouds gathered like an angry mob overhead and the ocean rose and fell in mountainous waves.

If the weather were to clear up, they would be able to see the islands of the Azores in the distance. But with the cresting waves and the low hanging storm clouds they could see nothing; they might as well have been entirely alone in the world.

Sarah Briggs was feeling sick. She'd been feeling sick for days, ever since the bad weather had rolled in. Married to a sea captain, she was no stranger to life at sea, but even so the constant rolling and tossing of the ship was getting to her. She was sat now, hunched over her sewing machine, trying to focus in the light of the lantern that swung violently from the hook above her head. She was trying to patch up a hole in one of her daughter's gowns; little Sophia had caught it on one of the ship's cleats last week and torn the hem clean off. Sarah dreaded to think how wonky the sewing lines would be when she looked at it finally in a steady light.

Little Sophia was asleep for the moment, bringing Sarah a blissful rest from trying to keep the toddler cooped up in the cabin. The first weeks of the voyage had been spent running blissfully up and down the deck. It was as though Sophia had been born to be at sea. But then the weather had rolled in. As the waves had grown and the sails had been lowered to protect them from the violent winds, she'd been forced to bring the child inside for fear that she would be swept overboard.

The circle of light swung forward again and fell on to the bed where Sophia lay amongst the sheets and blankets. Her arms were thrown wide in sleep, her head against the pillow with fine curls spread around her.

Distracted, Sarah was caught off guard when a particularly heavy wave hit the side of the ship and rolled the Mary Celeste almost fully onto its side. Sarah was nearly tipped from her chair and caught herself at the last moment by throwing out her foot and bracing herself against the nearby wall. She had thrown her arms forward and held the gleaming sewing machine fast against the table. With her arms full, the little bottle of oil she used to keep the cogs of the machine running slid sideways along the polished wood of the table and hit the floor with a tinkle of breaking glass.

At that moment the door to the cabin was thrown

open and the
roaring of the
wind and a spray
of rain burst into
the room. Her husband,
Benjamin, staggered in and
fastened the door behind him,
blocking out the relentless storm.

"Are you alright?" he asked, sweeping his sodden
hair back from his face.

Sarah steadied the table and crouched down to begin
gathering up the shattered glass from the vial, the spilt
oil dripping from her fingers and staining her skirts.
She sighed. "We're fine," she said, nodding towards the
crumpled bed where their toddler slept soundly, despite
the storm raging outside. Benjamin sank down to one
knee beside her and helped to gather up the scattered
shards.

"Benjamin," Sarah said at last, "how much longer will
this weather last?"

Briggs sighed and shrugged. "I just can't say. I'm sorry
Sarah. I can only hope that it won't follow us all the
way to Genoa!"

"I'm not sure how much more of it I can take." She
placed the broken glass into his outstretched palms and
clambered unsteadily to her feet as Briggs tipped the
pieces into the waste basket beneath his desk. "Poor
Sophia hasn't been outside of this room in days! I can
hardly keep down my meals."

Benjamin brushed his hands together and wiped the oil
on to a handkerchief whipped from his breast pocket.
He handed the cloth to her as he lent forward and
kissed her forehead.

"I'm sorry, love, I know it's hard. It's not what we had planned for the voyage! But take heart, the Mary Celeste is more than up to the job of carrying us through. She is a strong ship and a sound one."

He hugged his wife as the storm raged on outside, the wind howling through the sails and whipping the rigging into a chaotic drum roll. They could barely hear the cry that carried on the wind outside and it wasn't until Benjamin's second in command, first mate Albert, burst through the door without knocking that they realised something must be amiss. As Albert swung in the door, the full force of the storm crashed through behind him. The sheer strength of the raging wind sent the door crashing back against the wall, yanking the handle out of Albert's grip.

"Come quickly, Captain!" Albert cried over the wind. Behind him, a disembodied voice called from the deck.

"What was that?" Benjamin barked, still holding tight to Sarah's hand.

"Boz, Captain, he's been swept overboard. The storm is getting worse. It's growing stronger, Captain!"

Benjamin sprang into action, even as his child cried out, woken at last by the screaming of the wind. He kissed the back of Sarah's hand and let go. "Keep Sophia calm," he said. "All will be well - secure the doors and windows and for goodness' sake, stay in here!" And with that, he was gone.

Sarah held a hand to her mouth; Boz was one of the youngest sailors aboard the Mary Celeste, he was quietly spoken and undoubtedly one of her favourites to spend time with among the motley crew. She prayed that they would find him and pull him back to safety.

She crossed to the bed as the floor heaved beneath her, staggering at the last moment, and crying out as she banged her leg against the wooden frame of the bed. She scooped up Sophia, now wailing loudly, and held her tightly.

"Hush, it's ok my darling. Mummy's here," she soothed as she made her way unsteadily across to the window above the desk. The glass was thick and reinforced with strips of black lead and she'd often grumbled how little she could see out. Yet now she found herself grateful for the strength of that glass as the fierce wind and rain lashed against it with such force it sounded as though somebody was throwing stones. "It'll all be ok," she said again, steadying herself against the desk as she held her daughter tightly to her chest.

* * *

Out on deck, Briggs felt as though he too were being pelted by stones, without so much as a pane of glass to protect him.

"Man overboard!"

The words kept ringing in his ears. Edward and Andrew were desperately holding on to Volkert's arms, trying to stop him from hurling himself over the railings and into the churning sea after his brother.

"Do you see him?" Briggs shouted up to Gotleib, who clung for dear life to the rigging above and kept one finger pointing at the spot where he'd last seen Boz flailing against the waves.

"What happened?" Briggs demanded of Albert.

"A wave captain, it swept over the deck and took Boz away with it," Albert shouted. "We need to find a port - the ship can't take much more of this!"

Before Briggs could reply another faint shout came from above.

Albert shielded his eyes against the driving rain and squinted up at Gotlieb. He could see the boy shouting with all his might, but the storm snatched every word away and threw it out into the ocean. But through the rain Albert could see the boy, frantically pointing and waving his arm.

"Something on the starboard side," Albert called to Briggs, lowering his eyes and squinting over the railing trying to spot whatever Gotleib had seen.

A vast wave passed beneath the ship, tilting it first one way. The men clung for dear life to the railings, the rigging and the mast, before the ship flung itself back upright, almost hurling them loose. As the Mary Celeste fell into the trough of the wave, the dip between the mountain peaks, Briggs saw what it was that was causing Gotlieb such alarm. His stomach fell down into his boots; his knuckles white against the railing.

"Waterspout!" he bellowed, turning this way and that to make sure everyone and anyone could hear him. "Get below deck! Batten down the hatches!"

Looming out of the dark clouds like a cloaked demon, a swirling vortex of wind, fiercer than the one that already blew, a tornado was stretching down to the surface of the water below. As it reached ever lower towards the ocean the tornado began to whip up the water, sending the surface spinning around as though it were a whirlpool tearing through the stormy air.

"It's heading straight for us!" Edward shouted.

He let Volkert go and every man ran for the hatchway, dropping down below deck one after another. Briggs watched his men safely down as the tornado loomed ever closer, whipping water into his face so fast the droplets felt like knives. As the last man dropped out of sight Briggs hauled the hatchway closed, fighting with every ounce of his strength against the wind. But the tornado would have none of it; keeping up its steady rampage across the ocean, its funnel spiralling like a rope between the heavens and the earth. As the waves continued to roll beneath it, the base of the spiral, the spinning whirlpool, seemed to tumble down the side of the wave straight towards the stricken Mary Celeste. As the tornado crashed into the side of the hull the hatchway was blown entirely out of Briggs's hands and whipped away into the darkness. It was as though the tornado, with wind louder and stronger than he'd ever known, had thrown its shoulders against the side of the ship and was heaving with all its might to tip it right over, to capsize them to their doom.

Briggs crashed onto his back on the deck as it tipped and rolled, waves of spray and ocean water spat out of the tornado filled the open hatchways. He skidded along the deck and slammed against the railings, now so far tipped over they sat more like a floor. Ignoring the tempest that raged around him, threatening at any moment to hurl him to his death, he rolled onto his front and crawled across the railing, hand over hand. In front of him he saw a loose rope, flapping uncontrollably in the raging tornado, ripped from among the rigging. As the ship started to right itself, fighting with every ounce of its strength against the waterspout, Briggs leapt for the rope, wrapping his arms about it and dragging himself up towards the centre of the deck, the place where his cabin stood, almost fully on its side as it sheltered his wife and child.

As Briggs clung desperately to the flailing rope the power of the wind lifted him clean away from his ship and up into the air like a kite. He shut his eyes tight against the cutting water and felt objects slapping against him as he flailed through the storm, the flapping of the sails perhaps, or an unfortunate fish ripped from the ocean. Blindly, Briggs was flung around the mast of his own ship, like a ribbon tangled in a tree. And then, with a blow that knocked the breath from his lungs, the Mary Celeste suddenly righted herself with a jolt and Briggs crashed to the deck. Opening his eyes, blurry with sea water and his head spinning, he turned and saw the waterspout meandering away across the waves on the far side of the ship.

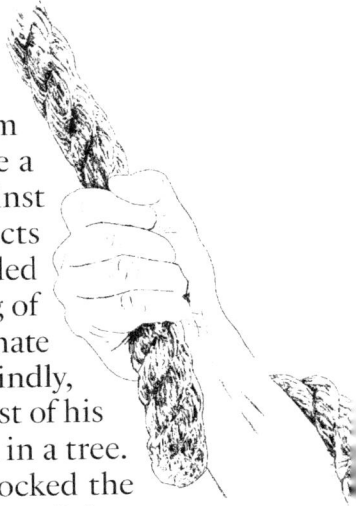

With shaking knees, he rose unsteadily to his feet, the wind of the storm suddenly seeming calmer than it had been for days. He looked in a daze around the ship, up at the tattered sails and the loose rigging. Across at the single lifeboat, the ropes fastening it down barely hanging on, one of its cleats torn loose. He saw the spare ropes, used for hoisting the now ruined sails, once neatly coiled against the deck, now strewn and tangled across the ship.

There was a split second of numb shock, of wonder at how the ship, his ship, had survived a collision course with a waterspout before he remembered Sarah. Dropping the rope that had saved his life he tore across the sodden deck and burst in through the cabin door. The whole room was a thoroughly wet mess, his papers scattered amongst the toys about the floor. The blankets and sheets of the bed were soaked through. Sarah's sewing machine lay on its side. The binnacle, the pillar of wood that held the compass, had broken. Something had evidently hit the glass compass case with such force it had smashed it in.

"Sarah!" he called, wading his way through the mess and further into the room. "Sarah!" he called again; his heart trapped in his throat. All the terrors he had been through that day, the waterspout ready to tear them apart, being hurled around the deck of his ship like a ragdoll, were eclipsed by the thought of losing his wife and child.

There was a cough from the depths of the room followed at once by the whining cry of a child. Feeling flooded back into his fingers then and he skidded to his knees and looked beneath the bed. Sarah, her hair bedraggled and messy about her face, peered out at him with a thoroughly miserable Sophia in her arms.

"Thank goodness," Briggs breathed, reaching under and pulling them both out, holding them in his arms as though he'd never let them go. Sarah was weeping in shock and relief and Sophia grizzled quietly between them. But the moment of peace among the chaos wasn't to last. Above the roaring of the waterspout that faded into the distance outside, they heard a shout.

"Captain! We're taking on water!"

Briggs pulled Sarah to her feet and sat her on the bedraggled bed. "Stay here," he said. "I'll be back." With that he turned and left the room.

On deck Albert was standing in the open hatchway, his

legs lost in the darkness below deck. His face was grim, his lips thin and white. "She's taken on water Captain, too much water. Come see."

Briggs clattered down the stairs after him, barely stopping to take in the destruction below deck, the steam that billowed from the doused galley fire, the hammocks all tangled and twisted, the pots and pans rolling about the floor. Arian sat on the closed lid of his chest, sadly poking at the soaked tobacco in his stash, completely unusable now.

Albert and Briggs pushed past and turned, dropping down the ladder and into the cargo hold. As Briggs reached the bottom, his feet splashed into cold water, rising up past his knees. He cursed and looked around at the cargo, hundreds of barrels, each of them full of industrial alcohol. Explosive, if left in the wrong conditions.

"Is the cargo damaged?" Briggs demanded, looking around at the flooded hull.

"Nothing out of place, Captain," Albert replied.

"I'll have the lads carry out an inspection though."

"Right," Briggs nodded. "Have you checked the sounding rod?"

Albert reached up onto the top of the nearest stack of barrels and pulled down a long wooden rod, which had notches carved along

its length and looked for all the world like a makeshift ruler.

"Is that it?" Briggs asked disbelievingly.

"The sounding rod is broken. I took apart the pump yesterday because of all this bad weather..."

Briggs rolled his eyes. "Well, there's no time to fix it now, this'll have to do."

Albert held onto the side of a barrel for support and waded his way carefully towards the centre of the hold, moving steadily as the ship still rocked in the wind and the unseen floor was uneven beneath him. As the Mary Celeste rolled, the water in the hold sloshed along with it, rising first up one side before rolling back down and crashing up the other.

Albert steadied himself as near to the middle as he could get and lowered the rod down into the water as far as it would go. Lifting it back out he counted the notches the water reached to. His face grim, he turned to Briggs.

"3.5 feet, Captain."

"Check again." Briggs ground his teeth. Three and a half feet wasn't the end of the world, but it was far from good. With the Mary Celeste already limping from the battering of the tornado, with her sails ragged and torn, if she was still taking on water then that spelt disaster. Albert braced his legs against the struts of the hull beneath the dark water and set his back against a huge barrel to steady himself before he lowered the rod back into the water again. Briggs held his breath.

"3.6 feet, Captain..." The two men looked at one another.

"It's going up?" Briggs said.

"Looks that way."

79

Their eyes locked, neither of them spoke. Between them passed an understanding borne of a lifetime spent at sea. The ship's hatches had been blown out; she'd been almost capsized. Who knew what damage had been done to the hull, hidden beneath the heavy barrels in the cargo?

"What do you want to do, Captain?" Albert asked, carefully making his way back to the safety of the stairs, gripping the sounding rod in one hand and holding tight to the ladder with the other. It was dark in the hold, but even in the shadows Briggs' eyes were bright with fear and panic.

"Launch the life raft," Briggs said. "Tell everyone we're abandoning ship."

"Captain?" Albert's mouth hung open. Leaving your ship in the middle of the ocean, in the middle of the storm, was perhaps the most dangerous thing a sailor could possibly do.

"You heard me," Briggs said. "We're abandoning ship. We'll tie the raft on a tow line, and we'll follow behind for a while. Then, if she goes down, we'll cut ourselves free and head for the Azores."

"But ..." Albert began.

"I said abandon ship, Albert. I'm not leaving my family on board this vessel for another second if there's even a chance she's going down. Don't panic man, it's only a precaution. If all is well and the water level holds, we'll be back on board within a matter of hours."

Albert swallowed nervously. He opened his mouth to speak, thought better of it and instead nodded solemnly to Briggs before turning and clambering back up the ladder.

Ten minutes later and the Mary Celeste's only life raft, a survivor of the tornado that had blown right through them, had been lowered onto the dark surface of the ocean. The waves might be calmer now, but the ship still rolled and the raft clattered against her side. Volkert, his face pale and his eyes red, and Andrew stood at either end of the raft, holding it fast against the Mary Celeste's side as the others clambered down.

They'd left all their worldly belongings behind on the ship. There'd not even been time to gather their pipes and tobacco. Sarah and Sophia had been the first ones into the boat, a small dripping doll clutched in the little girl's arms. They sat now at the far end of the raft, mother clinging to her daughter and huddled down against the bottom of the boat.

Soon Albert and Briggs stood alone upon the deck of the Mary Celeste. True to his word, Briggs had allowed Sarah to bring none of their belongings. If the sailors couldn't then she shouldn't either. There was a bundle of food supplies tucked safely beneath Edward's seat, and Briggs had the ship's sextant tucked with some essential papers beneath his arm.

"Check the tow line, and then down you go," Briggs said. Albert nodded gravely, but he didn't move at once.

Briggs reached up and patted his shoulder. "Don't worry, Albert, we'll be back on board before you know it."

Albert nodded grimly and moved forward, tugging and checking the knots of the rope that fastened the life raft to the ship were secure. With a nod to Briggs, he spun around and made his way down the ladder into the waiting raft.

Briggs gave one final look around the deck, desolate after the storm, everything waterlogged, hatches thrown off and the sails hanging like dirty laundry about the masts. He knew they would be back, probably before an hour or more had passed. He knew that. Yet somehow, he couldn't shake the sense of sadness he felt at leaving her behind. As though there was some slim chance that he and his sturdy ship might never see one another again.

"Daddy!" Sophia called impatiently, anxiously, from the raft. The sound of his daughter's voice shook him from his brooding and he too turned about and made his way down the ladder into the raft.

Edward and Andrew released their grip and pushed against the hull; inch by inch, the lifeboat drifted away from its mother ship. The thick brown rope that connected them to the Mary Celeste snapped tight and strained against the pull of the vessel.

The remaining crew huddled together. Captain, wife and child, all of them bundled into the bottom of the boat, their eyes locked on the Mary Celeste, limping alone through the choppy Atlantic waters. They watched as they were dragged along in her disorganised wake, every one of them trusting that the rope that tied them together would hold true. Every one of them wrong.

9

THE BEST OF A BAD BUNCH

"**A**h man," Max said, slumping back in his chair sadly. "Why have they all got to die in the end?"

"They didn't die!" Freddie corrected him. "They went off in the lifeboat."

"They're obviously going to die," Max countered. "You heard her at the end: 'Every one of them was wrong'!"

Alice smiled and gave a little curtsey. "See," she said. "No monsters, no aliens, no pirates. The explanation is

83

simple, they were caught in a storm, the ship damaged by a waterspout and Briggs ordered them to abandon ship as he thought they were going to sink. But of course, it didn't."

"That's even worse than mine," Gwen said. "So, the rope snapped and they all just drifted off to their doom?"

"Pretty much," Alice said bluntly.

"I think any story where everybody disappears, never to be seen again, is going to be sad, guys," Mr Lewes said. "But I think I know what you're all saying. Somehow drifting off alone into the ocean seems somehow worse than being quickly killed."

They each looked solemn and depressed at the idea.

"I don't know how Briggs could have made such a terrible mistake!" Gwen burst out. "Albert said himself, abandoning ship is probably the most dangerous thing you could ever do!"

"The ship was sinking!" Freddie said.

"But we know it didn't sink, don't we? So, he moved everyone into the life raft for no reason and then they all died!"

Mr Lewes nodded. "I can see why you might see it that way, Gwen, but it's difficult to know what we would do in his situation, with his wife and his baby on board."

"So, are you saying Alice's story is true? The Mary Celeste was hit by a waterspout, and they all jumped ship?" Max asked Mr Lewes, stunned.

"Now, I didn't say that exactly. I think Alice's story has a lot of strength to it. It takes into account a lot of the evidence."

"Like the sails," Alice said. "I read that people often think the ship was abandoned in perfect condition, with food still on the table and cups of tea still warm, but that's just not true. The ship was found in a pretty bad state, sails tattered and torn, water between all the decks and the hatches blown off. So, the waterspout idea explains all of that."

"That's true," Mr Lewes nodded. "I don't see much you've left out of your tale."

"Can we prove that the weather was bad at that time? Is there any way of knowing if there were terrible storms on that date?" Gwen asked. "I mean, we know the date of the last log entry, 25th November 1872, and we know they weren't far from the Azores islands. Surely there must be some evidence somewhere of a storm that awful?"

"It's a good point, Gwen" Mr Lewes said. "I have to agree with the others I'm afraid, Alice, I think I see some problems with your story. Why didn't Briggs write about all this awful weather in the logbook? I'm sure he didn't mention anything quite as awful as you've described, which, if it was damaging the ship, I'd have thought he would have."

Alice gave a shrug, unwilling to let go of her idea.

"Also, if the weather was that awful, why in a million years would he put everyone in a lifeboat?" Gwen said. "The lifeboat would have been tiny; they'd have no chance in a storm!"

"But if the storm was dying down, maybe you would," Alice countered. "Like Mr Lewes just said, we don't know what we'd do in that situation. If Briggs really thought the ship was sinking, I'm sure he'd get his kid off as soon as possible!"

"I think," Mr Lewes said, raising his hands for quiet, "as much as we might question Captain Briggs' choices that day, it seems to me that Alice's story is the best of a bad bunch. None of the theories you've presented quite work; none of them completely fit with the evidence that has been left behind. Clearly some of them were more exciting and thrilling than the truth probably was." He nodded to Freddie, Max and Gwen in turn, each of them grinned. "And others are far more possible than the rest," he said, nodding this time to Alice. "However, there is one more theory that none of you mentioned but which, I think, might hold up better than the rest."

They all sat up straight, intrigued, and looked eagerly at Mr Lewes.

"Are you telling us this isn't a mystery after all? That you just had us tell all those stories and you knew the answer all along?" Freddie was outraged, but Mr Lewes just laughed.

"Not quite, Freddie, calm down! I've got a theory that stacks up with a lot of the evidence found on the ship, if not all of it. But there is no way we'll ever be able to prove it for certain one way or another. The only way we could ever do that would be if Captain Briggs and his crew came back from the dead, or if his diaries washed up revealing secret information we can only guess at right now. So, the story I've got to tell is probably the best idea we'll ever have about what happened to the crew. It's backed up by a number of historians and scientists as well. So, why don't I tell you my version of events and then we'll see what you all think?"

The Clueless Club nodded, settled back in their seats, and prepared themselves for the Mary Celeste's final voyage.

10
Mr Lewes' Tale

Life on the deck of the Mary Celeste was normal. The November sun was rising slowly and the mist that cloaked the ship was finally lifting. The crew scurried about their tasks, like ants, each one busy with their own purpose.

A small child was crouched down, playing with a spinning top and begging her mother to watch. The toy rattled, wobbling uncertainly against the weather-beaten planks. A pair of sailors paused in their task of winding the ropes and cheered the little girl on.

Yet beneath their feet, below the deck on which the spinning top danced, things were anything but normal. With each boot that pounded across the planks, the vibrations rolled their way down into the hull.

Down in the darkness, a rat scurried along the ropes that held the barrels in place, stacked in rows three high. The creature's whiskers quivered, it could hear something at the far end of the hold and it could smell something awful. It approached with caution, its beady eyes long since used to the darkness of the cargo hold, its nose twitching as it moved, the smell growing ever stronger. The rat reached the end of the rope and drew up short; its snout wrinkled. The smell here was so strong, it threatened to overwhelm the tiny creature. Its eyes watering, the rat slowly backed up along the rope, one tiny foot placed carefully behind the other as it retreated cautiously. Now it was no longer scurrying noisily across the hold, the rat could hear the noise more clearly and through its watery eyes it could see the source, a blackness against the black. A steady, unerring drip, drip, drip, oozing from the three barrels stacked at the end. The droplets were landing in the shallow water that had gathered at the bottom of the hold and lapped gently against the bottom barrels. The liquid oozing out of the barrels wasn't water, however; the rat knew that much. No, whatever was leaking out was dangerous, even to the rat's simple mind. Those little droplets held some kind of lethal power. Even if it didn't understand why, it knew enough to be afraid. As the rat retreated, backing away from that endless dripping, from the suffocating fumes, there was a sudden rattling sound above deck, as a child's spinning top skipped its way across the floorboards of the deck above.

The first the crew of the Mary Celeste knew of the danger building up below deck was when the little girl gave a cry of surprise. The men scattered busily about the deck turned at the child's shrill shout. They saw mother and daughter stooping over something on the deck.

Albert, first mate and second in command of the ship, set down the ropes he was winding about his arms and crossed over to see what had drawn their attention. As he approached, he could hear the clattering of metal and saw the bolt that held the hatchway in place was jumping and fighting against the wood.

"What the devil?" Albert said, reaching out and pulling the child and woman back. The entire hatchway was dancing as though something within was desperately trying to escape, something that couldn't spend a moment longer down in that hold.

"My toy!" the little girl whined as Albert picked her up and thrust her into her mother's arms, her spinning top left to knock feebly against his boot.

"Get her back to the cabin," Albert ordered her as he waved frantically for the other sailors to join him. As one, they downed tools and gathered around the hatch, that still clattered and jumped against the restraint of the bolt. Its nails were beginning to work their way free with the force of the vibrations.

"Volkert," Albert said, his eyes glued to the phenomenon, "check the other hatches. Arian, get the captain. Eddie, you come with me. Everyone else, keep her sailing until we know what's going on."

"Is it meant to be doing that?" Gotleib asked, his accent thicker than usual in his fear.

"No," Albert replied darkly.

"Where are we going?" Eddie asked, his great, hulking shadow falling over the hatch way.

"The other hatches are secure!" came Volkert's shout from across the deck, only just audible over the clattering of the bolt.

"We're going to find out what's down here," Albert said grimly. "When I say go, flip the bolt."

"You sure?" Eddie didn't sound convinced, and Albert looked up at him, unnerved to see his giant of a friend chewing on his lip.

"Just do it," he snapped. "Now!"

Eddie reached out, trying to keep his body as far from the hatchway as possible, and slammed the bolt free. There was an explosion of noise and fumes and rats. The two men were thrown back against the deck as a cloud of black smoke rose up into the sky and vanished on the wind. As they landed heavily on their backs, the smell of alcohol washing over them like a physical presence, burning the hair from their nostrils, they were swamped by hundreds of rats. Many of them charred and burnt, their fur in flames and smoke trailing along behind them as they squealed in fear and pain.

As Albert and Eddie staggered to their feet, kicking and flailing at the vermin, the other sailors jumped up the rigging like monkeys.

"What the devil is going on?" Briggs bellowed, marching over and staring wide-eyed at the swarm of rats that was spilling from the hatch, fleeing across the deck and tumbling beneath the railings into the sea.

All along the side of the ship, countless little splashes could be heard as each rodent plopped into the ocean to their death. Whatever it was they were fleeing was clearly worse than the certain death the Atlantic offered them. Here and there a little hiss erupted as a rat, its fur still smouldering from whatever flames had overcome them, hit the water, and sank beneath it, cool at last.

"Good God," Briggs breathed. He turned to see Volkert running back across the deck, tripping blindly over the dropped ropes as he watched in horror as the last of the rats threw themselves over the side of the ship to their doom, their tiny corpses bobbing around the ship like corks.

"What's that, man?" Briggs barked, looking at the wooden pole Volkert held clasped in his hand. The pole had notches carved along its length like a ruler and the lower half was dark with water.

"The sounding rod, Captain. I checked the main hatch; it was secured. But I decided to check the sounding rod and, well look, Captain." Volkert held out the rod.

"Three feet! Curses!" Briggs cried, throwing the stick aside. "What's going on Albert?"

"An explosion Captain, in the hold. You smell that?"

"Of course I smell it," Briggs snapped, his fear turning to anger. "There's no soot! How could there have been an explosion with no soot?"

"There was smoke," Eddie butted in. "A huge cloud of it when the hatch blew open."

"The rats were on fire, Captain," Gotleib added from

behind them.

"Are we sinking?" It was Brigg' wife, cradling her toddler in her arms, the girl still crying for her lost toy.

Briggs looked at her without speaking. He blinked once before turning to the sodden rod in Volkert's hands, the water mark showing just how much water the Mary Celeste had taken on. He moved his feet, following the trail of ash and dust the rats had left in their wake.

"Launch the raft," he said in barely more than a whisper.

"Captain?" Albert asked, laying a hand on Briggs' shoulder, his face a picture of horror and disbelief.

"You heard me!" Briggs shouted. "Launch the raft - now. Sarah, get whatever you need but bring only what you must. The rest of you, leave your things here."

"Abandoning ship?" Albert hissed, pulling Briggs around and forgetting all sense of respect and obedience. "Are you mad?"

Briggs seized Albert's wrist and threw it from his shoulder. "I am not mad, Albert! And I could have you thrown off my ship for speaking to me in such a manner. The rats leaving the hold, throwing themselves overboard, that was enough for me. But that God-awful smell! It's burning my nose and eyes. Whatever has caused the water in the hold and the hatch to blow off - I'm not sending a man down there to check and I'm not waiting to see if the rest of the ship is about to blow! Not with my wife and daughter on board. So no, Albert, I am not mad, I'm keeping my family and my crew safe. We will abandon ship in the raft, but we'll keep her fastened on and we'll trail behind her until we're sure the air has cleared, and no further explosions or disasters befall her." Albert shook his head in disbelief.

"And then, Albert, and then when all is well we will simply pull ourselves back to her side and continue on our way. But not until I am certain that it is safe to do so. Rats flee a sinking ship, Albert. Rats flee fire and danger and death. I will not wait around here to see what fate they chose death in order to avoid!"

He gripped Albert fiercely before pushing him back. "Now go, get Sarah sorted and ready to disembark."

Albert looked Briggs dead in the eye, his expression dark and blank. Then with a tense nod he spun on his heel and followed Sarah into her cabin. Briggs shielded his eyes from the rising sun and looked up onto the roof of the cabin, where his sailors were lowering the one and only life raft down a makeshift ramp and lowering it over the side. Each man coughed from time to time and paused to waft the air in front of his face, trying in vain to clear those acrid burning fumes that billowed up from the hold through the open hatchway. As the sailors started throwing ropes and essentials into the boat, Briggs marched past them and entered his cabin. He paused a moment at his desk, looking down at the open logbook, he'd barely even finished putting in the date before the commotion had erupted on deck.

The only words: *25th November 1872.*

He gave himself a shake. He'd be back to finish the entry before he knew it. He snatched up the map of the area, crumpling it in his haste, and stuffed the sextant into his pocket. Heaven

25th November 1872

93

forbid they should need it, but it would be wise to keep themselves aware of their location as the Mary Celeste drifted rudderless in the ocean. He took one last look around his cabin. He couldn't quite shake the feeling that now, this very moment, was significant. As though all the days of his life had been leading up to this moment and finally, it had arrived. He sighed, ignoring the sensation of hurtling towards a fate that he hoped only to avoid, and turned from the room.

When he arrived back on deck, coughing and gagging as he passed through a cloud of those sickening vapours, he saw that his men had already lowered the liferaft into the water. His wife and daughter were huddled up in the stern of the boat, blankets across their laps and a doll clutched in Sophia's pudgy little arms. Briggs tossed his things down to Albert, who stood with one foot upon the edge of the boat and a fist holding her firmly against the side of their ship, the ship that, until this morning, had carried them safe and true along their course.

"Is everyone aboard?" Briggs called down to Albert.

"Aye, Captain. All present."

Briggs nodded and turned, keeping his eyes averted from the deck he'd vowed never to abandon, from the one haven of safety and security in this wide and dangerous ocean, and clambered down the ladder. As he dropped into the boat beside Albert, his first mate turned to him, his voice low so the others wouldn't hear.

"Are you sure you want to do this, Captain?"

Their eyes met, and the two men stood there a moment, the waves lapping against the sides and splashing back against them from the hull. Both men exchanged a hundred words in their silence; both knew the danger and the folly of abandoning your ship and putting your faith and trust into a lowly lifeboat, praying only that it would keep you afloat on this tempestuous ocean.

"Set us loose," Briggs said. "Get us as far away from her as possible."

With a grim nod, Albert pushed against the side of the Mary Celeste and let their little raft drift away from her. The rope, fastened tightly to their prow, started to unravel from the deck of the ship, giving them more and more line and allowing them to drift further and further behind their ship. Soon they were far enough away to see the whole of her, gold letters spelling out her name.

"So strange," Sarah murmured quietly from the back, "to see her from so far away, yet still at sea."

No one replied. There was a gentle jerk as the rope reached its end and snapped tight, pulling the craft through the water in the wake of the ship.

"It won't be long," Briggs said in a brave voice, light with pretended jollity. "It won't be long, and we'll be back on board. Let's just give the girl time to settle and clear the air."

There were scattered nods from the crew, but the expressions were sombre and dark, almost as dark as the clouds that were stirring up behind him, bringing in a storm to swallow them up into oblivion.

11
NOT SO EXCITING, BUT JUST AS SAD

The classroom was silent. The ticking of the clock above the door was the only sound as the children looked at one another.

Freddie broke the silence. "Well..." He closed his mouth again and frowned.

"It's not a nice way to finish the investigation, is it?" Mr Lewes said, dropping down onto the chair behind the teacher's desk and leaning back. "Drifting off into the abyss."

"It was all for nothing as well!" Gwen was frowning again, a deep furrow creasing between her eyebrows.

"What do you mean it was for nothing?" Mr Lewes asked.

"Well, the ship didn't explode, did it? We know that because it was found a week later, totally undamaged. So Briggs made them all leave the boat and sent them all to their doom for nothing!" Gwen folded her arms angrily, as though Captain Briggs had personally offended her.

"I think I'd have gotten off," Max said fairly. "If the rats were jumping ship, I certainly wouldn't have hung around to find out why!"

"The rats were made up though, right Mr Lewes?" Alice looked at her teacher, who chuckled under her accusing gaze. He held up his hands in surrender.

"Fair enough, I'll admit the rats were a bit of creative licence to add some drama to the tale. It may have happened, but there was no evidence of it. The rest of the tale, however, is generally agreed by many authorities to be the most likely scenario."

"You said "most" authorities agree," Freddie cut in. "So you're saying we can't rule out the Kraken then?"

"The pirates were better," Max mumbled.

Alice rolled her eyes. "It's not about which one is the best story, it's about which one is true."

"You're all right," Mr Lewes said. "We arguably can't rule anything out, but there is definitely some compelling evidence to support the alcohol explosion theory."

"Like what?" Gwen asked.

"Well, for starters one of the hatches was found, upside down alongside the opening. As though it had been thrown off. It's true, the main hatch was still secured in place, however, the explosion may have burst out of the weakest point.

"It was also noted by the investigators who assessed the ship when the crew of the Dei Gratia finally sailed her into Genoa, that ten of the barrels in the hold were empty, undamaged but empty, as though the contents had simply leaked out somehow, which could have caused the build up of fumes that caused the explosion."

Mr Lewes looked at the four faces, all of them crumpled in thought. Max opened his mouth to speak, and then closed it again. Mr Lewes waited patiently, until at last Max said: "But that's ridiculous, there was no ash or scorch marks when Deveaux looked around, there can't have been an explosion!"

Mr Lewes smiled as though he'd been hoping one of them would bring up that thorny issue.

"Funny you should say that, back in 2006 a chemist at University College London actually recreated a replica of the Mary Celeste's hull and ran some experiments. It turned out that when the leaked alcohol fumes were ignited by a spark, a ball of flames went upwards and amazingly, not a single one of the barrels was left charred or burnt, in fact there were no signs an explosion had even happened."

"That's crazy!" Max exclaimed. "How does that even work?"

"I'm no chemist," Mr Lewes said, holding up his hands. "But the way I understand it, the fumes created a kind of pressure explosion that left no damage behind it but would have, for example, blown the hatch of a ship off."

"That would have been terrifying," said Gwen solemnly. "Especially if there was a ball of flames bursting out of the hatch!"

"I know, right! I'd be jumping ship, that's for sure," Freddie said.

"So there we have it, the mystery of the Mary Celeste, solved," said Alice. "The Clueless Club wins again!"

"Indeed! You should all be very proud of your theories and stories, it's been quite a night of adventure and fear!"

"So, now that case is closed, what's next?" Max said, as the others began gathering their bags and coats together.

"Well, next week we'll be sticking with our nautical theme, but we'll be moving a bit closer to land this time. Your homework is to investigate the case of the missing lighthouse keepers of Eilean Mor."

"The missing lighthouse keepers of where, sorry?" Freddie asked.

"Eilean Mor, it's a small rocky outcrop that makes up part of the Flannan Isles off the northwest coast of Scotland. In December 1900 there were three men tending the lighthouse there, keeping the light running. The men would stay on the island for weeks at a time with no contact from the outside world. When a boat arrived at the island on 26th December ready to relieve the men, they found the lighthouse completely abandoned."

"What happened to them then?" Freddie demanded.

"Well that, Freddie, is the question and I very much hope you'll all be telling me the answer next time!"

THE END

You've read some of the theories, now it's time to come up with your own. What do you think happened to the crew and passengers of the Mary Celeste?

Use the next pages to plan and write your own story about what you think happened.

What do you think happened?

What evidence supports your story?

-
-
-
-
-

Timeline of events

Add the events and scenes from your story to the timeline below to help you plan out your chapter.

Think about:

- Where does your chapter start?
- Who will your main characters be?
- Using 'wow' words to help you build suspense
- How will you give your story a dramatic finish?

Start

End

X

Title:

_____

_____
_____
_____
_____
_____
_____
_____
_____
_____
_____

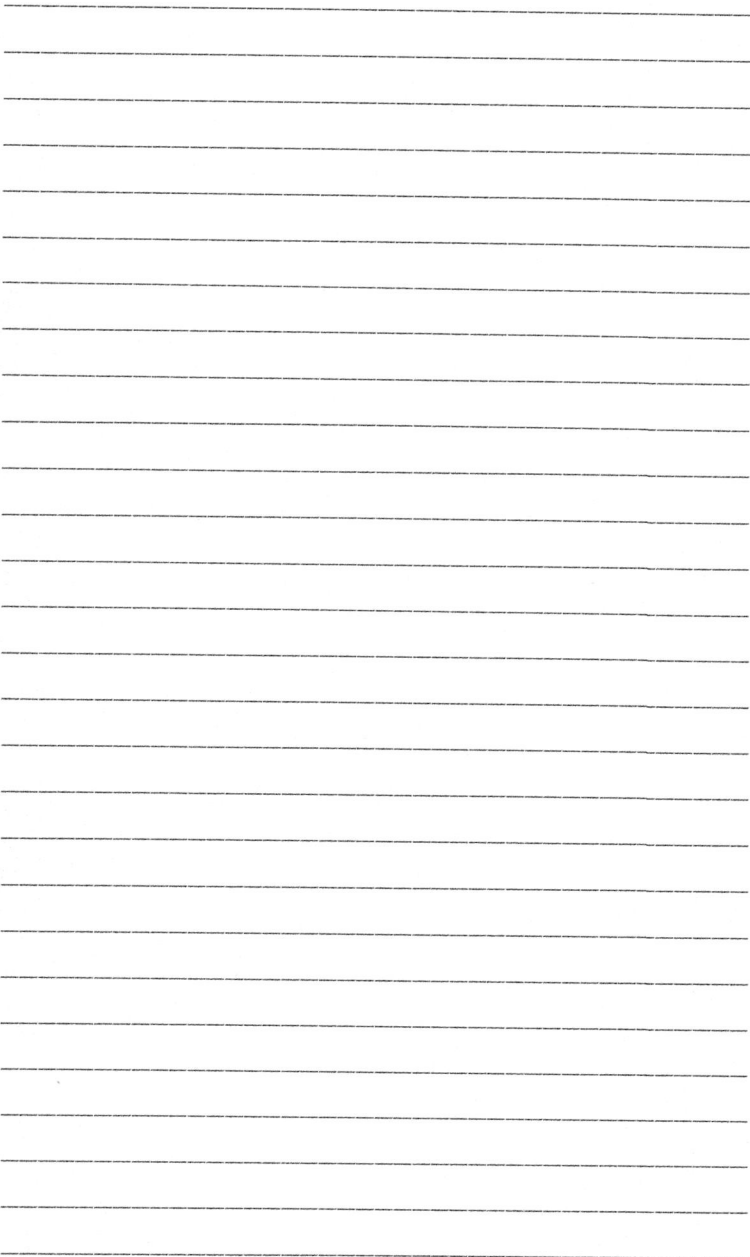

Why not share your story with us for a chance to see it published on our website?

Visit **thecluelessclub.com** to email us your story.

WANT TO KNOW MORE?

Whilst researching for this book I came across a lot of websites that contained incorrect information about the Mary Celeste. Over the years, many writers have dramatised the mystery, including the author of Sherlock Holmes, Arthur Conan Doyle. These wonderful fictional tales, while fun and exciting, have led to lots of false information getting mixed up with the facts. For example, you may read that there were half-eaten meals still warm on the plates when the Mary Celeste was discovered. This sadly isn't true!

With this in mind, be careful when finding out more about this topic. If you need some help, ask a teacher or adult to help you out with your research.

SOME BOOKS AND WEBSITES I FOUND HELPFUL

• Britannica and Britannica Kids

• The Smithsonian Magazine

• The University College London blog

• **The Story of the Mary Celeste**

– Charles Edey Fay

• **Mary Celeste: The Greatest Mystery of the Sea**

– Paul Begg

IN THE NEXT BOOK:

TAKES ON
THE MISSING LIGHTHOUSE KEEPERS OF EILEAN MOR

Join the Clueless Club as they take on the mystery of three missing lighthouse keepers on the Scottish island of Eilean Mor.

From sea beasts to ancient curses, and from rogue waves to murder, the mystery is as creepy today as it was when the keepers vanished from their uninhabited island over 100 years ago.

Visit
thecluelessclub.com
to find out more!

About the Author

Amy lives on the Welsh border with her husband, three daughters, Merlin the dog, Bagheera the cat, three feral chickens and Little John the cockerel.

Amy spent most of her career bringing history to life in the classroom for KS2 students. She now works for an exciting prosthetics start-up supporting children with upper limb differences. Despite all the distractions, she's always been a writer and THE CLUELESS CLUB TAKES ON THE MARY CELESTE is the start of her first published series.

Talk to Amy about history, board games, mysteries and dinosaurs if you want to lure her into a conversation. She obviously has a favourite dinosaur and she'll probably ask you about yours!

Lauren is a London-based illustrator who designs stylish and fun patterns to jazz up prosthetics for people with upper limb differences, like Clueless Club member, Gwen.

She loves being outside in nature, standing atop mountains (but not necessarily climbing up them!), gazing at the moon, doing yoga and drinking coffee. She almost always has her film camera on her and has a reputation for baking the best cinnamon buns in the West. Lauren is also very proud of her Duolingo streak of over three years learning Italian (per favore, non metterlo alla prova!)

You can see more of Lauren's designs, and her minor obsession with the moon, on her Etsy store:

www.etsy.com/uk/shop/LaurenWDesign

Thank Yous

Thank you first and foremost to my long-suffering husband, Benedict, who has endured twelve years as an intermittent writer's widower. While you've never had a choice per se, you've always listened diligently and with minimal complaints whenever I *have* to read the latest chapter out loud - regardless of the time of night or whether you'd been asleep or not.

To Diane for diligently and patiently reading every one of my books multiple times to weed out the many errors and for never once criticising my general incompetence with paragraph formation to my face.

To Lorna and Orlie, for being the first ever readers of 'The Clueless Club' and for your thoughts and feedback. To Theo for being one of my best students and first readers, and also for your boundless enthusiasm when it comes to history and the Kraken.

To Nina, for giving it to me straight and pushing me – *finally* – to turn this book into a reality. To Masters, for forever being my writing champion. To Taz for always being keen to read my latest offerings and seeking out typos with an attention to detail that would make Sherlock proud.

Thank you to my partner in mystery and my colleague in prosthetics, Lauren, for trusting in my writing enough to bring your artistic talents on board and for breathing life into my stories with your drawings.

Last but obviously not least, to my eclectic, loved and loving family. To Mummykins for fostering an adventurous spirit in me. To Dad and Di, for your unwavering encouragement of my pursuits. To Lauren, Matt and Ellen for the love, laughs and the late-night dances. And finally, to &Co, the world's best employee.

Amy

xx

THANK YOUS

To my family for always encouraging me to pursue my creativity and never once telling me to pick a more academic path, and especially to Mum for pushing me to finish the projects I start. It really is worth it!

To Esmé for being my fresh set of eyes when I need constructive feedback about proportions, expressions and all things illustration, I will forever value your opinion. Thank you for being a model that one time (see 'feedback about proportions').

And to Amy for trusting me to bring your writing alive with my illustrations. I am honoured that you asked me to work with you and I appreciate your patience as I work outside my comfort zone. This truly is the most exciting project and I cannot wait to create more!

Lauren
xx

Printed in Great Britain
by Amazon